Our Journey With Jesus

A story of God's amazing goodness, provisions and guidance.

Pastor Don Bergstrom

Our Journey With Jesus

OUR JOURNEY WITH JESUS
ISBN: 978-1-60416-883-9

Copyright © 2013 Don Bergstrom
All rights reserved.

No part of the material protected by this copyright notice may be reproduced or used in any form or by any means, electronic or mechanical, including photocopying, recording, or by any information storage and retrieval system, without the prior written permission of the copyright owner.

First Printing May 2013

Reformation Publishers
242 University Drive
Prestonsburg, Kentucky 41653
1-800-765-2464
rpublisher@aol.com

Printed in the United States of America

Don Bergstrom

Preface

My wife, Debi, and I were married on Saturday, October 20, 1973. Before saying *I do* to each other, we had already determined that we would strive to walk through this life following the footsteps of Jesus. Since that day, He has been there to provide for us and to guide our pathway. Several verses from the Bible have especially shaped my Christian life.

First, Proverbs 3:5-6; *Trust in the Lord with all your heart; do not depend on your own understanding.* **Seek his will in all you do, and he will show you which path to take** *(New Living Translation).* A second verse is found in Ephesians 2:10; *For we are God's workmanship, created in Christ Jesus to do good works, which God prepared in advance for us to do.*

Over the years, as we began to share stories of God's goodness and grace, people began telling me that I needed to write a book. After thirty-six years of preaching and teaching, our good congregation in Houston, TX, gave me a three-month sabbatical. When I finally decided that this really was a gift

Our Journey With Jesus

from God, it seemed to be the perfect time to get away and write. So here I am in Shawnee, WY, hiding out at our daughter and son-in-law's ranch, putting down on paper what has been building in my heart for all these years. All Bible verses come from the New International Version unless otherwise noted.

Don Bergstrom
Houston, Texas
May 1, 2013

Don Bergstrom

Dedication

This book is dedicated to my mother, Ruth Mildred Bergstrom. When she moved to heaven in 1998 we found a note in her Bible. It included her testimony and her life's purpose. She stated that, although she had *done nothing great for God*, she believed that her purpose was *to raise her seven children in the nurture and admonition of the Lord (see Ephesians 6:4)*. I, of course, am one of those seven children.

We all grew up, married, and had children of our own. And those children had more children. Today that family tree bears more than 130 names. At least 120 of them are serving Jesus Christ. Among them are pastors, youth pastors, worship leaders, Sunday School teachers and parents who are still raising their children in the *nurture and admonition of the Lord.*

Thanks, mom, for remaining faithful to your call.

Our Journey With Jesus

Table Of Contents

Chapter One - *Beginnings*	7
Chapter Two	9
Chapter Three	12
Chapter Four	14
Chapter Five	24
Chapter Six	28
Chapter Seven	52
Chapter Eight	61
Chapter Nine	65
Chapter Ten	72
Chapter Eleven	74
Chapter Twelve	76
Epilogue	82

Chapter One
Beginnings

Debi and I met on a Friday night in the spring of 1973 at Soul's Harbor Church in Minneapolis. We had both grown up in Christian homes, but at that time I was not fully committed to Jesus Christ. The Sunday before we met I had attended a Lowell Lundstrom concert at Soul's Harbor and was invited to return that Friday evening for the launch of their new Young and Free singles' ministry. I drove up in my 1971 Corvette Stingray, while Debi had walked many blocks through the rain to attend their first Sundaes on Friday event in the basement of the church. Although she was a student at North Central Bible College in Minneapolis, Decatur, IL, was Debi's home.

Debi walked in just seconds after I had arrived and we met in the church foyer. She was soaking wet but I sure thought she was good looking. I said something like, *Well, I guess this must be the place. Yes, it is,* was her reply. Unimpressed, she headed for the restroom to dry off a bit before the meeting. We didn't speak again for a few weeks. I mistakenly thought she was with a guy named Tom, and I wasn't about to get in the way of that romance.

I began attending Soul's Harbor quite frequently on Sunday evenings. One night an evangelist from Canada, Brian Ruud, was speaking. The Holy Spirit spoke through him and I ended up at the altar where I surrendered my life completely to Jesus Christ.

I also became a regular face at the weekly singles' ministry meetings. One evening, as I was preparing to leave the church and head to Altman's Cafe where the group often gathered after Bible study, I noticed that Debi was all alone in the foyer. I bravely asked if she needed a ride to Altman's. She accepted my offer, and we sped off together in my Vette.

Later I learned that Tom was just a friend and that she was not dating anyone at the time. I drove into Minneapolis a few nights later to see her again, and she invited me to attend an Andrae Crouch concert at Soul's Harbor on Friday evening. That was our first official date. Following the concert we were among a select few who were invited to a quaint little deli to meet with Andrae for a bite to eat. What an honor that was for me!

I returned to Minneapolis on Saturday to help Debi move out of her dorm room into a tiny apartment that she planned to share with another North Central student. On Sunday morning I drove into Minneapolis again to attend church with her. On Sunday afternoon she came back to Buffalo with me and spent the night in my parents' home. On Monday (Memorial Day) we drove up to Lake Superior for the day so I could show her some of the places I often went with my family in my younger years.

That week we saw each other several more times, and soon we were practically inseparable. By midsummer she was offered a great job in her hometown of Decatur, so she headed south, thinking she would return to North Central that fall. However, God had other plans.

Chapter Two

. . . you cannot become my disciple without giving up everything you own. - Luke 14:33,
New Living Translation

During our time apart, I attended a Sunday evening service at Soul's Harbor where Winkie Pratney was speaking. He challenged those who were serious about following Jesus to lay everything on the altar; our hearts, our past, our present, our future, our plans, our possessions, and our relationships. I came forward and gave God everything I had, everything I was, and everything I ever hoped to be. Little did I know that Debi was attending a similar service more than 500 miles away. Independently that evening, to the best of our understanding, we were both now totally committed to the God we would spend the rest of our lives serving.

One of my prized possessions that I presented to the Lord was that 1971 Corvette Stingray. Several days later I was ready to crawl into that car to head for work. I heard the Lord speak to me! No, it was not an audible voice, but I knew it was Him. He asked, *Do you love me more than you love this car? Of course I do, Lord! Don't you remember my commitment last Sunday evening?* He was silent.

The next morning I had the same experience! My reply was the same. And the third morning? Same question from Him, same response from me. Then I heard Him say, *If you love Me more than you love this car, then I want you to sell it!*

Tom, the guy I thought Debi was dating, drove a Porsche, and he always said it was God's car. So I called him. *Does your Porsche still belong to God? Yes, of course*, was his reply. *Well, my Corvette belongs to Him, and He just told me to sell it.* Tom explained that this was my Isaac moment. God, he said, was asking me to sacrifice my car on the altar of obedience (see Genesis 22:1-18). *Once God knows you meant it when you gave the car to Him, He will, in effect, give it back to you.*

To prove my supreme love for God, Tom suggested that I put an ad in the paper for three days offering to sell the car. At the end of three days God will be satisfied. Tom's words seemed to make sense, so I put the ad in the Minneapolis Star and Tribune. On that Friday morning, before the ink was even dry in the newspaper, I received a call from an interested buyer. Within two hours he came to look, took the car for a test drive, and wrote out a check for the asking price. When I called Tom to let him know what had just happened, I think he got a bit nervous! I began to realize that, when I gave everything to God, He took me at my word!

Another thing that Debi and I had independently laid on the altar those few days earlier was our relationship with each other. So now, if we were going to see each other again, it would be up to God. Well, soon He did confirm that this relationship could continue, so on Labor Day weekend I drove to Decatur with a ring. She accepted it! Before the weekend was over we set a wedding date of October 20, which was just seven weeks away. Our thinking? *If this is of the Lord, what*

are we waiting for? We married on a Saturday night in Buffalo, MN, in the Evangelical Covenant Church I had grown up in.

That evening after the reception died down we sped away on our honeymoon. When we checked into the honeymoon suite, the guy at the counter asked how many were in our party. What was he thinking? The next morning I checked out our car carefully, knowing how my family and friends were prone to find honeymooners and make their lives miserable. Sure enough, I found a dead fish and some limburger cheese on the manifold of our Pontiac Grand Prix. After about 5 wonderful days, I called home to see how things were with our family business. When I learned that my brothers were swamped and could probably use my help, we turned the car north and headed for home. I promised Debi that I would make it up to her at a slower time of year.

On the way home we stopped in Bloomington, IN, to have dinner with Debi's aunt and uncle, Darold and Carolyn Harris. Before we continued our journey north they asked, *So, what has God called you to do with the rest of your lives?* They also reminded us of a Bible verse found in Ephesians 2:10; *For we are God's workmanship, created in Christ Jesus to do good works, which God prepared in advance for us to do.*

I was quite sure I knew the answer to that question. I would return to our retail family business, teach Sunday School, tithe and raise a Christian family. At least that worked for my dad! Then they asked, *Is that your plan...or God's?* I sure didn't have an answer, but I did remember that not many months earlier, I had presented even my share of the family business to Him, along with my future.

As we drove out into the night, I couldn't shake their question. Debi and I began to pray, reminding God once again that everything belonged to Him and that we were ready to serve and follow Him completely. What He created us to do is certainly what we were willing to do.

Chapter Three

Go, sell everything you have and give to the poor ... Then come, follow me.

- Mark 10:21

Take my life and let it be
Consecrated, Lord, to Thee.
Take my silver and my gold,
Not a mite would I withhold,
Not a mite would I withhold.

Our first two years of marriage were great! Debi found a job, the family business continued to prosper, on March 28, 1975, our first child, Michelle, was born, and we were doing everything possible to get out of debt, something we believed God wanted us to do.

We also became involved in the life of the church, leading a Bible study for young adults in our home. Two single guys came to Christ in our home and, through prayer and the Bible, we were able to help several young couples through some of life's struggles. Although I was fully committed to the family business, it was becoming increasingly exciting to come home at night to see what God would do next through our growing ministry there.

In 1975 we began to hear His voice again. *Sell everything you have and give to the poor ... Then come follow me!* After months of fasting, praying, listening to Him and seeking counsel from our pastor, we made that decision. In late 1975 we began to sell and give away everything. Whenever we sold something, we used the funds to get further out of debt. Once that was accomplished, we began giving everything away under the Holy Spirit's direction.

Don Bergstrom

In March of 1976 our second child, Jason, was born. Since we had even given up our medical insurance we wondered prior to his birth how we would pay for such an event.

One day, while visiting a post office, I noticed a literature rack placed there by the Civil Defense people. One little brochure was about emergency childbirth. I sensed the Holy Spirit prompting me to take a copy. As we talked, fasted and prayed about this possibility, Debi and I had to wrestle with the fact that the baby could come breach, she could die, and I could go to prison! We soon made our decision. The brochure gave accurate information and the grace of God was present as Jason was born. Debi and I had just experienced our first home birth. A few people called us foolish, suggesting that we were now the ones testing the Lord! Although we are not against medical insurance, doctors, midwives and hospitals, for us this was just one more step in our faith journey. We have always taught and believed that, *If Jesus brings you to it, He will see you through it!*

By that fall the only asset we had left was our home. Our mortgage balance was $25,000 and it was on the market for $35,000. Although real estate sales were slow, a man from our church approached us with an offer. He would give us his Holly Park mobile home valued at $10,000 and then take over our $25,000 mortgage. It sounded good, so we accepted the offer. Several weeks later our pastor made an announcement one Sunday morning. A new youth pastor would arrive in a few weeks. The only missing piece was housing. Since his salary would not be huge, the pastor suggested that someone in the church might have an over-the-garage apartment that they would be willing to rent at a decent price. Debi and I looked at each other, wondering if a mobile home would provide adequate housing. Soon we were signing the mobile home title over to the church. We were now homeless, penniless and unemployed! *Lord, here we are – ready to follow You!*

Chapter Four

And my God will meet all your needs according to his glorious riches in Christ Jesus.
                                                    - Philippians 4:19

We moved in with my parents as we waited on His direction. Since we had sold and given away even our cars, we couldn't go far unless God would provide transportation. An unexpected $400 insurance refund showed up in the mail. After giving $40 back to Him, I felt Him prompting me to take $300 and go car shopping. A Volkswagen seemed to be what He had put on both of our hearts, so I began combing through the newspaper for a bargain. I soon learned that for $300 I could buy a VW that had a blown engine. Another choice was a total rust bucket, and yet another had been converted into a Baja Bug. I began to doubt God's knowledge of used car prices down here on earth. In fact, I was downright discouraged after a day of car shopping!

My wife picked up the newspaper, and noticed that there was a '68 VW Bug for sale that I had not circled, crossed off, or written a note by. *Deb, you don't understand! A '68 has the 12 volt system and high back seats! Those are selling for around $2,000, and we've only got $300!*

Debi replied, *Well, it says make offer.* Soon she was on the phone with the VW owner's wife. *Yes, my husband will be there within the hour to make an offer.*

Debi, I'm tired, the car is at least 40 miles away, and there's no way they'll accept our offer! She just smiled as my brother's fiancé drove me into Wayzata to look at the car. Debi has never been pushy or overbearing, but when she knows she's right, she will take a stand. As my future sister-in-law and I entered the neighborhood where the Bug's owner lived, the homes were huge! As we rounded the final corner I saw the little white VW sitting in a driveway – next to a new Cadillac El Dorado! I was sure that this was a wasted trip! But as we got closer to the home, I sensed His voice saying, *that's your new car!* Wow, it was a cute, clean, low-mileage beauty! As the owner came out of his front door, he was offering me the keys so I could take it for a test drive. I'm thinking, *if this is God's choice, I don't need to drive it!* In fact, with my limited resources, I didn't want to waste any gas that might be in the tank! I did fire up the engine, looked it over real good, and then prayed for boldness!

So…you're here to make an offer? Yes, I stammered, *I am here to make an offer…of $300! Okay, I'm willing to hold the car for a few days with a $300 deposit…if you can pay the balance before Friday.*

No, you don't understand. My total offer is $300! Now *that* made him laugh! *$300 for this jewel? Do you have any idea what it's worth?*

Yes, probably around $2,000. But I don't have that kind of money, so I'm offering $300. He was no longer laughing! *Hey, pal, I have a friend who's a banker. I'll let you have the car for $1,800. If you've got any kind of job at all, with your $300 down payment I'm sure he'll give you a loan for the other $1,500.*

No, I don't think he'll give me a loan…because I don't have a job. It was *then* that he began to call me a few names I cannot repeat, and asked why a guy like me was unemployed! *Well, I was in business with my family, but my wife and I just gave everything away. We're going into the ministry!*

Now his face was getting red and his voice was getting louder. *SO, I SUPPOSE YOU'RE GOING TO TELL ME THAT **GOD** TOLD YOU TO BUY MY CAR FOR $300!*

Well…sir…yes… that's a good way to put it.

Our Journey With Jesus

By now he was yelling at me! *DO YOU SEE THIS CADILLAC? I'M IN SALES...AND I HAVE PAYMENTS TO MAKE! AND I'VE SPENT FAR TOO MANY NIGHTS WAITING AT HOME FOR IDIOTS LIKE YOU TO COME AND LOOK AT MY VW! I SHOULD HAVE JUST GIVEN IT AWAY TWO WEEKS AGO – BECAUSE I'VE LOST TWO WEEKS OF EVENINGS WHEN I SHOULD HAVE BEEN OUT MAKING SALES! AND NOW YOU COME AND INSULT ME WITH A *%#@%&!&* OFFER OF $300?*

Now his wife was out in the driveway, begging him to calm down! *What will the neighbors think? WELL, THIS BOZO IS TELLING ME THAT GOD SENT HIM TO BUY THIS CAR FOR $300!*

Well, dear, if God sent him, you'd better let him have it. Maybe that's why we haven't been able to sell it sooner. As he stormed off into the house, his wife signed the title over to me, took the $300, and wished me well.

I drove away in shock! I think I was even trembling a bit, because the guy with the Cadillac was big enough beat me up pretty good! But as I left the neighborhood, I began to praise the Lord for the miracle of the VW! The car was just the right size for Debi, Michelle, Jason and me. Since we had given everything else away, the diaper bag and a few extra clothes fit inside the car without any problem.

We soon headed for Bloomington, IN, to see Debi's aunt and uncle. They were traveling around with their ministry of personal evangelism. We began to travel with them while we waited for the Lord to open the next door. Since I was an introvert without any formal training, I certainly knew that God had not called me away from the family business to preach! My role, I was sure, would be to serve in some capacity behind the scenes. Perhaps I could drive a bus for Bill and Gloria Gaither. An even more exciting possibility was that I could perhaps fly an airplane for Missionary Aviation Fellowship!

Don Bergstrom

Meanwhile we continued to serve with Debi's aunt and uncle. We had also been driving our VW for a number of months and it was a very reliable, economical car! One night while we were in Decatur, IL, we were invited to a Bible study on the university campus. Since we rode with Debi's aunt and uncle in the back seat of their car, we had no idea where we were going. At the end of the Bible study, the leader asked us to form a prayer circle and share our prayer concerns with one another. A young woman next to me said, *I am praying for a car.* The leader asked if I (a stranger to the group) would pray for her request. But before I could utter a word, she added, *I'm praying specifically...for a 1968 Volkswagen! May I ask why? Yes, my sister has one, and her boy friend knows how to keep it running.*

Since that made sense to me, I began praying a faith-filled prayer. After all, I certainly knew that God was able to provide a '68 VW! About half way through my prayer, I sensed the Spirit saying, *Give her the car!* I ignored the prompting and finished my pious prayer.

That night I couldn't sleep. As I tossed and turned, Debi asked what was wrong. *I think we were supposed to give our precious little car to that young woman.* Debi had been sensing the same thing! The next morning Debi's grandma offered to take us to Bob's Big Boy Restaurant for breakfast. As we sat there, grandma looked at me and asked, *are you okay? You've really been quiet this morning.*

We told grandma what had happened the night before. She reminded us that, if this was God's plan, then we should probably give the car away. As I was making all kinds of excuses (like, *I have no idea what the young woman's name was, where she lived, etc*), Debi stopped me and pointed toward the door. Sure enough, the young woman I had prayed for the night before was walking through the front door of Bob's Big Boy!

Our Journey With Jesus

Reluctantly (I really liked that car, and surely didn't have another $300 to buy another one) I walked over to the young woman who immediately recognized and welcomed me. To make a long story short, I signed the title and agreed to deliver the VW to her just as soon as we could remove our few belongings.

Oh, great! Now what will we drive, I thought, as we walked from the college campus back to grandma's house. It was quite a hike – but I was thinking we ought to get used to walking! Before that day was over, Debi's aunt and uncle showed up and gave us their old Ford Econoline Van! It had recently been repainted and had been converted into a camping van – complete with a bed inside, and plenty of room for our kids!

Since that day back in 1977 we have given away more cars than I can count (including that Ford van), but God has always provided another vehicle. Some have been more exciting than others, but He has always been faithful!

Following Him eventually took us to Boulder, Colorado. Believing we were to go there, we lived in our conversion van for a while, waiting for direction. One Sunday morning we visited a small Nazarene Church near the University of Colorado campus. We were warmly greeted and when the service was over a family invited us to have lunch with them. They had many questions about who we were, why we were in Boulder, etc. Following a delightful afternoon together, they invited us to return for their Wednesday evening Bible study. We continued to worship with them for the next several weeks. Then, following one Wednesday evening Bible study, the congregation was urged to remain for a special called business meeting. We were asked to wait in the lobby until that meeting was over. Soon we were called back into the sanctuary where the meeting was being held.

The church was without a pastor so their parsonage was empty. Their insurance company had earlier contacted the congregation, concerned because this empty home was an open invitation to vandalism. So, *would we be willing to move into that parsonage until a new pastor was called? And,* in exchange for a free place to stay, *would we be willing to begin a ministry for young adults from the college?*

We moved out of our van into the parsonage that very evening. What a blessing that was! We also began a Thursday night young adult gathering that rapidly grew to about 30 in weekly attendance. Soon the young adults were hanging out at our new home more often, and we began to see some of them making commitments to Jesus Christ. During this time bags of groceries would often show up at our door, and friends and a few family members began to send limited financial support.

One Sunday morning following the worship service at the Nazarene Church, the chairman of the congregation asked if I could preach next Sunday, since their interim pastor would be out of town. I explained to him that I did not feel called to preach. Remember, I was the introvert who wanted to drive a bus for Bill Gaither!

Well, if you're not a preacher, would you be willing to teach one of your Thursday night young adult Bible lessons to all of us - from the pulpit? What could I say?

Sunday morning came and I was a nervous wreck. I gave it my best and then invited the congregation to respond at the altar. Three people gave their hearts to Christ that morning, including two of the young adults from our Thursday night gatherings. I was amazed, and knew it was *only* because the Holy Spirit was at work that morning.

Eventually a new pastor was called and it was time for us to move out of the parsonage.

We moved into an apartment to continue this new ministry. Finances were limited, but God always provided the rent and a bit more. Well, I should say, He provided *most* of the time!

Our Journey With Jesus

December's rent would soon be due and the flow of finances had strangely slowed to a trickle. So I came up with a plan...

From day one we were convinced that, if God had called us and if God was leading us, we would never have to beg or even ask for money. But I decided to write a Christmas letter and send it out to everyone we knew. I would not *ask* for anything, but in the letter would *thank* those who had supported us, subtly letting *everyone* know that we depended on the gifts from a few to live! No, I was not asking anyone for anything, but sure found a way to *hint* that we needed more supporters!

I had tons of copies of that Christmas letter run off at Kinko's and addressed envelopes to everyone I could think of! All I needed now was stamps. Many stamps! Debi had set aside the last of our money for groceries. I convinced her that, if she would allow me to *invest* her grocery money in stamps, the return would be phenomenal! By 6:00 p.m. that day all of our Christmas letters had been dropped off at the post office, and now all we had to do was wait for the blessings to come rolling in!

The next morning the post office called. I knew it was too soon for us to pick up a truck load of cards, so I waited to hear the reason for the call. Well, during the night, vandals had blown up the drop box (the one I had dropped our Christmas letters in) and they were now trying to piece return addresses together so they could call all those who had deposited mail in the box the evening before. Our Christmas letters had been blown to smithereens! If we could tell the postmaster how many letters we had dropped off, they would reimburse the cost of the stamps - with more stamps!

So our letters were gone and Debi's grocery money had been reduced to stamps! Many stamps! Meanwhile the family was getting hungry. I decided that my bright idea had not come from God. So I got alone with Him and began to pray about our financial dilemma.

Don Bergstrom

Once again I heard His voice. There was someone from my past that I needed to forgive and God was using this financial shortage to get my attention! Out of desperation and obedience I wrote a letter to this person (remember, I had enough stamps to do this). I confessed my part of the offense and asked for his forgiveness. I dropped the letter off at the post office (this time I went inside), and sensed that God's will had been accomplished. Soon the mail carrier came by our apartment to make his daily delivery. To my delight, we received tons of Christmas cards from friends and family that very day, including some financial gifts! I paid our rent and replenished Debi's grocery fund.

On Christmas Eve there was a knock on our door. When I opened it, a number of saints from that Nazarene Church entered with gifts for our children and bags of groceries for all! I now fully understood that God had used our situation to teach me a valuable lesson: **sin leads to want, but obedience leads to blessing!**

Dear reader, is there some unanswered prayer in your life? Is there an unmet financial need? Psalm 66:18 says, *If I had not confessed the sin in my heart, the Lord would not have listened... (New Living Translation).*

By the end of January God would use a second financial lack to teach me another valuable lesson. Since we didn't have money for gasoline, on Sunday morning we visited a rather large church closer to our apartment. The sermon was taken from 1 John chapter three. When the preacher came to verse 17, I really sat up! *If anyone has material possessions and sees his brother in need but has no pity on him, how can the love of God be in him? Dear children, let us not love with words or tongue but with actions and in truth!*

Now, *that's* the kind of love we really needed that day! When the morning service was over, a young couple thanked us for our visit. The husband asked, *Gonna watch the Super Bowl today?*

No, was my reply. *Guess you're not into football* he said. *Well, actually I can't watch it because we don't have a T.V.* He wondered if this was a moral choice we had made because of our Christian convictions.

No, we don't have a TV because we can't afford one! In fact (here I was *subtly asking* again) *we don't even have any food in the cupboard today.*

I was thinking that, after the sermon we had all just heard, this would be a perfect opportunity for this couple to demonstrate some of that Biblical love by inviting us over for food and football! Even though my comments were now *more than* subtle, no such love came our way. I was still learning to let God control our circumstances!

The next morning I walked back to the church where the receptionist warmly greeted me. I explained that we had visited the church the day before and loved the sermon. She agreed that, yes, it was a wonderful, Bible-based message! That's when I told her why I was back. We were in need of food, and I was hoping for a demonstration of yesterday's exhortation from the pulpit. She then informed me that only the senior pastor could authorize a distribution from their food pantry and this was his day off. When I suggested that I might come back tomorrow, she informed me that, since it was staff meeting day, catching the pastor could be difficult!

Wow, what kind of place was this? It appeared to me that no one was practicing what was being preached! Since I still had yesterday's bulletin, I walked to a nearby phone booth outside of a gas station (remember phone booths?). I looked up the pastor's name and address. After asking the gas station attendant how to get to this address, I walked the short distance to the pastor's home. I was going to get food from this church

Don Bergstrom

one way or the other! I rang the doorbell. Soon the pastor opened the door just a crack and asked me if he could help me.

I visited the church yesterday, and loved your message! And I was wondering if my family and I could get the kind of love you spoke about. You see, we have no food!

Are you a Christian, he asked? *Oh, yes sir. In fact, we are seeking God's will for a lifetime of ministry!*

He then quoted Psalm 37:25; *I have never seen the righteous forsaken or their children begging bread.* He went on to tell me that, since I was begging bread, I had either just lied to him about being a Christian, or else there must be some great sin in my life that was preventing God from providing, and he was not about to get in God's way! And with that, the pastor of that large church shut the door in my face! I was shocked! How could God allow such hypocrisy?

As I got alone with God, trying to sort all of this out, once again I heard the Holy Spirit speak. First, He commanded me to forgive the young couple, the receptionist and the pastor. He was using them to teach me another valuable lesson! The Holy Spirit went on to say that *one day I would be in a position to welcome strangers into my home, and one day I would be in a place where the hungry would come to my door.* The lesson?

Now that you know what rejection feels like, do not ever turn them away! For, I tell you the truth, whatever you did for one of the least of these brothers of mine, you did for me (see Matthew 25:40).

Since that day, many strangers have come to our door seeking help and many hungry have approached us with their needs. By His grace we have never forgotten the lessons learned in Colorado.

Chapter Five

Unless a kernel of wheat falls to the ground and dies, it remains a single seed. But if it dies, it produces many seeds.
- John 12:24

Although ministry was taking place in Colorado, I still had no idea what God was calling me to do for the rest of my life. I was spending much time in His Word and in prayer but there was no clear direction for our future. Then we sensed the Spirit telling us to make a trip back to Minnesota. Along with seeing family and friends, we also stopped by the church to see our former pastor, Rev. Don Thomas. He asked how our ministry was going. When I explained to him that not that much was happening and that no clear direction was coming for our future, he nodded as if to say, *Yes, and I know why.* He opened his Bible to John 12:24 and read to us the words that you see above. He also took us to Galatians 2:20; *I have been crucified with Christ and I no longer live, but Christ lives in me. The life I live in the body, I live by faith in the Son of God.*

Pastor Thomas explained that, before I could live a spiritually fruitful life, I had to die to self. He also explained that, if I would completely die to self, the Holy Spirit would gladly fill me, and then use me for God's glory. One more verse fits into the conversation we had that day. Speaking of Jesus, in Matthew 3:11 John the Baptist said, *But after me will come one who is more powerful than I, whose sandals I am not fit to carry.* <u>*He will baptize you with the Holy Spirit and with fire.*</u> I asked Pastor Thomas how to die to self. Since he had another appointment, he simply told me to *pray for a funeral and then pray for a filling.*

Once we returned to Colorado I got alone with God and began praying for that funeral.

Don Bergstrom

The Holy Spirit began to reveal to me that, even though I was a Christian, and even though we had forsaken every earthly possession so we could follow Him, I was still trying to run my life my way. One example? I repeatedly had told Him that, since I was an extremely shy guy with no formal training, *I could never, and would never, preach.*

As I poured out my heart, I once again surrendered everything to Him. *Lord, if you want me to preach, I will preach. Where you lead, I will follow. Where you send, I will go. Whatever you ask of me, I will do without question.*

And the filling? Many denominations and movements that embrace a Wesleyan-Arminian theology teach a second work of grace. Some call it a baptism with the Holy Spirit, others refer to it as being filled with the Spirit or being entirely sanctified.

As I continued to pray that day, I eventually felt a peace within that I had not known before. I had given Him all of my demands and all of my desires. Although I knew that the Holy Spirit was a resident in my life, I now invited Him to become the *President* of my life! There was no manifestation or sign. Yet I was confident that self had been laid on the altar, that His Spirit had answered my prayer, and that He had filled me to overflowing. In the words of an old Dallas Holmes song, I was no longer the one in the driver's seat of my life, but was ready to leave *all* the *driving to the Chief.*

Some years later I read Dr Arlo F. Newell's book, *Receive the Holy Spirit.* Here's how he describes what had happened to me that day:

> <u>The extent of saving grace goes beyond the initial forgiveness of sin to the sanctifying of our very nature by the infilling of the Holy Spirit.</u> Many persons, having been born again, find themselves struggling with divided desires, undisciplined appetites, and strained interpersonal relationships. While having found a

*forgiveness of sin, they have not been able to find the peace of God that is available through the Holy Spirit. Questions arise, like, Must I continue this war within? Is there no peace in Christ other than this knowledge of forgiveness? Does he only save me **in** my sin? Or can I be set free **from** my sin? While not a panacea for spiritual ills, holiness does provide an answer to these questions, for all of them deal with the wholeness that can be ours.*

*Paul, having experienced this struggle in his own soul, wrote to the Christians in Thessalonica. Without question, he affirmed that this experience of holiness is God's will for every believer (1 Thessalonians 4:3). God has called us not only to conversion but to the wholeness of holiness (4:7). Being concerned for these Christians whom he loves, Paul prays: And the very God of peace sanctify you wholly; and I pray God your whole spirit and soul and body be preserved blameless unto the coming of our Lord Jesus Christ (5:23). The use of the word **wholly** is indicative of the completeness of his work of grace. Having experienced new life in Christ through being born again by the Holy Spirit, the believer finds within a hunger for holiness. Redemption has restored in the creature the image of the Creator. Now the desire is to do his will and become more and more like him in true holiness. A quest for more of God's likeness brings each person to a deeper experience of diving grace.*

Dr Paul S Rees, beloved world Christian, has said that "too often we have become connoisseurs of terms, rather than consumers of truth." He is correct in that too often we place the emphasis on terminology rather than theology . . . <u>Of this we may be sure, there is a crisis experience in the Holy Spirit beyond initial conversion which makes possible the wholeness of the child of God</u> . . .

Don Bergstrom

The first-century church experienced this complete filling of the Holy Spirit. While being made possible by the blood of Christ (Hebrews 13:12), this sanctification (setting apart) was the result of divine human interaction, involving the human will to consent and God's power to sanctify. Dr Ralph Earle says, "The common usage of the two terms leads us to affirm that a human consecration is the prerequisite for a divine sanctification." <u>Consecration is more than an emotional response to a religious ecstasy. It is the instantaneous, willful, decisive act of surrender on the part of God's child - forevermore yielding every avenue of one's being to the control of the Holy Spirit.</u> Such a commitment does not end with one glorious moment, but is a continuing, growing experience of obedience to God's will. While claimed instantaneously by faith, it is to be lived out progressively. While beginning with a crisis, it is also a process in spiritual development.

This crisis experience in the Holy Spirit, this consecration, this act of absolute surrender, this commitment spoken of by Dr Newell, is what I experienced that day in Colorado. In response to my hunger for more, the Holy Spirit filled me to overflowing. And, although He's still working on me, I have sought to keep in step with the Spirit since that day (see Galatians 5:16-18, 24-25).

Chapter Six

Whether you turn to the right or to the left, your ears will hear a voice behind you, saying, "This is the way; walk in it."

- Isaiah 30:21

When our ministry with the students in Colorado came to a halt because of their summer break, we began to pray for a new direction. A few years earlier Debi's parents had moved to Texas where they *thought* they would take over *Little Israel Ranch*, a place where troubled youth lived. We sensed that we were to move there, and believed that it would be to help her parents re-launch this ministry. That re-launch never happened. However, the church they were attending asked if we would give them six months of our lives to begin a ministry to young couples. Like so many of America's churches today, there were a number of women attending without their spouses (who were off fishing instead of assuming their place of spiritual leadership in their homes).

Although the church really had nothing to offer in return, they *did* promise that we would always have a roof over our heads and that we would never go hungry. Ben and Janice were among the first we would minister to. It had been our privilege to pray them into the Kingdom, and now we were striving to teach them how to do marriage and family God's way.

One Sunday morning the battery in our car died, so we walked to church. Since we only had $5.00 to our name I knew we couldn't buy a new car battery, so we decided to give it to God through the morning offering, knowing that He would find a way to take care of us. As we began walking home after the worship service, Ben and Janice stopped to give us a ride. When I explained to them that we were not walking for our health (especially since it was very hot and Debi was very pregnant again), but we were hiking home because of a dead battery, Ben asked if we should stop by the auto parts store for a new one. I once again humbled myself and told them that we had no money for a new battery.

Once back home, Ben wanted to take a look under the hood of our car. Maybe our problem was as simple as a bad battery connection or a battery that needed water. Once we agreed that it was shot, he said he would buy a new battery for us. Praise the Lord! Meanwhile, Debi was taking care of our kids and Janice had decided that Ben and I needed some ice water. Remember, it was a hot Sunday in Texas, and it was even hotter under the hood of that car! When she opened our freezer to get some ice, she noticed that all we had in our freezer *was* ice! She then peeked into the refrigerator, and was a bit shocked to find that it was also very empty. As she delivered the ice water, she whispered something into Ben's ear.

We headed for the auto parts store where Ben bought the best battery they had. Then we stopped at the local H.E.B. grocery store. I assumed that Ben was loading up two grocery carts (with steaks, milk, fresh fruit, expensive bread, breakfast cereal, ice cream, etc) for them. No, it was for us! I'm glad we gave our last $5.00 to God that morning! Once again He was taking care of us!

While still in Texas, on July 29, 1977, our third child, Rebekah, was born. She was our second home birth. Prior to her delivery we had heard many horror stories of children being born with the umbilical cord wrapped around their necks. Sure enough, as Debi was pushing and I was waiting to *catch* Rebekah, the cord was wrapped around her neck! We prayed in earnest as I carefully unwrapped it. Thank you, God, for another miracle!

I was spending some of my time helping Rev. Ben Campbell turn an old bank building into a worship center. His plan was to eventually plant a church in that former bank

Our Journey With Jesus

building. One day he asked if we would *help* him plant that church. Our task would be to form and oversee a youth group and also run a Bible book store that was to become a part of the ministry. Although Ben and I worked well together and although this seemed like a great open door for us, we began to pray and fast, asking the Holy Spirit to speak concerning this opportunity.

In our spirits Debi and I kept hearing the word *OREGON!* We had never been there and had no idea why we should ever go there, yet that seemed to be a clear voice from Him. Isaiah 30:21 says it this way: *Whether you turn to the right or to the left, your ears will hear a voice behind you, saying, "This is the way; walk in it."* It was *this* voice that we sought to hear.

On the fourth day of the fast we were both convinced that we were not to stay in Texas, but instead were to head for the Pacific Northwest. Wanting to be absolutely sure, we asked God for just one more clear confirmation. As I was painting the interior of what would become the new sanctuary, a stranger walked in and asked for Pastor Ben. He was out running errands, so I asked if I could help this stranger. He said, *When Ben returns, just tell him that I stopped by...and that **Oregon** is the place to be.*

Although this was just another man, in that moment his voice somehow sounded like the voice of God! To us, it was the final confirmation that we had been asking for!

Soon we were on the road to Oregon! Several days later, it was early Sunday morning as we headed west on I-84. Coming down the hill into Pendleton, we decided it was time to stop and find a worship service. Debi pointed off to the south side of the freeway, noting that there were two steeples at the next exit. Hoping one of those churches had scheduled a potluck that day (we were about out of money again), we prayed...and then headed for the Pendleton Church of God. Because there are several groups that have adopted this name, and because we had never visited any of them, we wondered if we might even find snake handlers inside! We would soon discover that, although this group with headquarters in Anderson, IN, believed in God's power to heal and protect, they did not believe in testing God through snakes!

As I looked through the bulletin, I noticed that no potluck was scheduled. Oh well...God usually fed us, so we weren't going to worry about lunch just yet. Following a great worship service a woman invited us to her home for lunch! Hallelujah! Turns out, she was the pastor's wife! After lunch we sat and talked.

The pastor wondered who we were, where we were coming from, and where we were going. We didn't have many good answers! We explained that God had called us, and that right now we were just learning to walk by faith while we waited for His clear direction.

Pastor Wayne Woodworth was preaching a series of sermons on faith. Since we were striving to live what he was preaching, he asked if I would share a thirty-minute version of our story in their Sunday evening service. As he introduced us to the congregation, he admitted that he didn't know us well, but sensed that we were to share our story. So we did. At the end of our testimony Pastor Wayne had one more prompting. He asked the congregation to participate in a love offering for us. Praise the Lord! Now that we had money in our pockets again we planned to continue traveling west. However, because it was late, the pastor and his wife invited us to spend the night.

On Monday morning we were packing our few belongings back into the car when Pastor Wayne approached me. Could we go for a walk? *Sure.*

Next door to his home was a duplex that looked like a real project, including cracked windows and broken down fences. He explained that the duplex came with his house and that he needed to get it fixed up and rented out soon. Was I a handyman? Could I do anything with the mess? Free room and board was offered in exchange for work on the duplex, so we accepted his offer.

For forty days and nights I worked on the rental property – patching sheet rock, painting walls, fixing windows and fences, cleaning carpets, repairing leaky faucets and more. On day forty-one we put up a *For Rent* sign and before the day was over, I had rented both sides of the duplex out for Pastor Wayne.

During many of those long evenings when Pastor came home from meetings or hospital calls he would come to the duplex to check on my progress. As we sat on old paint buckets, he would also ask me about my beliefs and convictions. He wanted to know what I believed about the Bible, the Trinity, the Holy Spirit, salvation, and much more.

One night I turned the question around and asked him what *he* believed. He said, *I'll let you know when we differ.* Then he asked if God was possibly calling me to serve Him through the Church of God. He told me that my convictions aligned with theirs, and that there was a tiny church 40 miles away in Milton-Freewater, OR, that was looking for a part-time associate pastor. There would be no pay, but the church would provide an apartment for us! God would have to take care of the rest!

There were 13 people left in the church when we arrived. A nasty split some months earlier had taken its toll. My duties included Sunday evening services, Wednesday evening Bible studies, ministry to their small youth group, an occasional hospital call, and visits to former members who might be willing to return. Since the interim pastor lived some 40 miles away I was the church's leader during the week. During those months the church began to grow. And God really was providing for us in some very unusual ways – including groceries on our doorstep, gas that somehow filled the tank of our car overnight, and money that folks were led to give us.

One Sunday morning a young man named Rick surrendered his life to Christ. Since he had tons of questions, I suggested that he join us for lunch. That way we could talk all afternoon! He explained that his clothes were in a washing machine at a nearby laundromat and he needed to go there first to finish that task. He promised to be at our home for lunch within an hour or so. Debi then informed me that we had very little food. So, what did I think we should serve Rick for lunch? Actually, we were down to one can of corn and one can of green beans...and tea bags! Wow! We began to pray for a miracle! Remembering that Peter could not walk on the water until he stepped out of the boat (see Matthew 14:25-29), we decided to set the table, put on the corn, and boil water for tea. That's when the doorbell rang. Thinking it was Rick (and hoping that he liked corn and tea), I opened up the door.

No, it was not Rick. Instead it was an elderly couple from the Church of God in nearby Walla Walla, WA. That morning their pastor, Howard Baker, had preached a similar sermon to the one we had once heard in Colorado, However, Pastor Baker had closed his sermon with an exhortation to go out and put God's Word into practice!

Since this couple had heard about the new associate pastor in nearby Milton-Freewater, OR, and since they also knew that the congregation was small, they concluded that we could probably use some food. So, after leaving their church that morning, they stopped at the nearby Safeway Store and loaded the trunk of their big Chrysler with groceries! So here they were, standing at our door, asking if I could help them unload this treasure! There were steaks, a big bag of potatoes, bread, butter, milk, fresh fruit, breakfast cereal, more corn, ice cream, and so much more!

Our Journey With Jesus

By the time Rick arrived, the steaks were almost done, the potatoes were almost baked, the bread and butter were on the table, and the corn was about ready to eat! After stuffing himself, Rick rubbed his belly and with a big grin concluded that, *If all pastors ate like this, maybe he should become one!* Several weeks later we finally told him what had really happened that day.

One morning our daughter Michelle asked if we could get a TV. She had spent time with another family from our church and was apparently impressed with this luxury. I gently explained to her that, if she wanted a TV, she would have to ask Jesus. Then, if He wanted us to have one, He would have to provide it. She toddled back to her bed, got down on her knees, and began to pray for a TV. A few minutes later she came out of her bedroom, got up on the couch and began to look out the window. She stated that she had prayed, and that Jesus had promised to provide. Wow! What should I tell her NOW? She had done what I had suggested and was now stepping out in faith! While I was scrambling for the right words to explain that *sometimes Jesus says yes, sometimes He says no and sometimes He says wait,* the phone rang. It was Bertha from the church. They had just been to K-Mart and found a colored TV on sale. Could we use their old black and white model? If so, she would be by in just a few minutes!

As their little blue Datsun station wagon was pulling up, my phone rang again (which caused me to be unable to run out and help with the TV). As Bertha was unloading it, Michelle calmly said, *Well, I guess Jesus got Bertha to deliver our new TV.* With answers like that, I was ready to turn my entire prayer list over to Michelle!

I spent one Monday working on our federal income tax return. In spite of our meager income, since we had not paid any taxes throughout the year, we now owed the IRS $73. We didn't have it! On April 15, I waited for God to provide it.

Sometimes financial gifts would come through the mail, and I was convinced that this would happen that Monday. But when the mail carrier finally showed up around 3:00 p.m. there were no gifts! I began to fret! What was God doing? Certainly He would not want us to be late in paying the IRS! Besides, He *always* provided whatever we really needed on time!

As I paced the floor praying, in her own gentle way Debi asked if I had a stamp. *No, I don't have a stamp* (the ones from Colorado were really gone). *Well, when God provides the $73, you won't be able to mail the tax return because you don't have a stamp. Why don't you take a step of faith and go buy a stamp?*

Since Debi often has more wisdom than I do in these situations, I decided to go and buy a stamp. On the way out of our apartment complex I ran into Larry Jackson, a new Junior High band teacher in town who was now attending our church. He flagged me down in the middle of the driveway and asked, *Hey, I've been wondering... how do you guys live? I mean, the church is not large enough to support a family your size...so how do you live?*

God provides, was my short answer – even though at that moment I wasn't so sure. *Well, does He sometimes provide through other people?* I assured Larry that, yes, He often does. *Good*, said Larry, *that confirms what I believe He wants me to do! You see, I just received my income tax return and sensed that I was to double tithe! Ten percent to the church and ten percent to you!*

By now there were several cars lined up behind mine so I needed to move on. Recognizing that fact, Larry shoved a check through my car window and said, *See you Sunday.* I glanced at the check...and of course, it was made out to me in the amount of $73.00! I rushed to the bank to deposit it – then sped off to the post office to buy that stamp so I could send in our tax return!

Our Journey With Jesus

One Monday morning we needed to make a trip to Portland, OR. When I parked the car on Sunday evening, the gas gauge was on empty. We had no money for gas, yet we were persuaded that we needed to make this trip on Monday!

Since our Provider had always been faithful, we set the alarm for 3:30 a.m., trusting that He would figure out how to get us to Portland. When that alarm went off we got up, got dressed, and I carried the first of our three children toward the front door. Since I did not want them to wake up, I left the lights in the living room off. I planned to put them in the car, hoping they would continue sleeping for the next few hours on the road.

As I opened the door into the darkness of the early morning, I was shocked to see someone standing at our door! And the person at the door seemed shocked to see me as well! It was Bertha, the *free TV woman* from our church. What was she doing at our door at 4:00 a.m.? My first thought was that something had happened to her husband, Howard, but for that she would no doubt have called us.

After we both got over the shock of seeing one another at my door, I invited her in. She explained that, for the past several months she had been saving up for an expensive blender for her kitchen. Since they lived on small Social Security checks, having this blender was a big deal. However, for the past several nights she couldn't sleep because the Holy Spirit was telling her to give the money she had already saved up to us! But she was wrestling with the Lord over this. At 3:30 that morning, Howard, who also couldn't sleep because of her tossing and turning, looked at Bertha and said, *Well, why don't you just get up and give them the money! Maybe then we can both get some sleep!*

So here she was at our door, having another wrestling match with the Holy Spirit. She had determined that she would give us the money, but now she wondered if she should really ring our doorbell at 4:00 a.m. and wake us up! So when I opened the door (fully dressed and carrying a child), she really *was* shocked to see me!

That's when I reminded her that we needed to make this trip to Portland. She handed me a wad of bills and then asked if we needed to take all of our children with us. If we would allow her to just crash on the couch, she would watch the children until we returned home later that day. Done!

As Debi and I crawled into our car, she was praising the Lord for the money that would fill our gas tank! But I reminded her that we still needed a miracle - because the closest gas at 4:00 a.m. was more than 30 miles away, and the fumes in our gas tank surely wouldn't take us that far! *But,* Debi exclaimed, *the gauge says full!* Thinking the gauge must be stuck, I pounded on the dash to free it up. Then Debi reminded me that it couldn't be stuck on full since it hadn't been even close to full in weeks. I jumped out of the car, opened the little gas door and stuck my finger down the filler neck. And, sure enough, I struck fuel! I ran back to our front door and caught Bertha just before she crashed.

Bertha, thank you again for the money...but how on earth did you fill our gas tank? She was clueless! To this day, I still have no idea how our gas tank got filled - especially since the car key was in my possession all night! In the Bible there's the story of a poor widow whose supply of flour and oil was supernaturally replenished throughout an entire famine (see 1 Kings 17:7-16). What God had done for her He had no doubt just done for us! When we returned home later that day, I tried to give Bertha the money we had not used for our journey. She refused. No more sleepless nights for her! After she went home, Bertha learned that her neighbor had held a yard sale over the week-end. One of the unsold items was a brand new blender still in the box! It had been a duplicate wedding gift but had not sold on this yard sale. Since Bertha had been such a caring neighbor, would she like to have it? It was even better than the one Bertha had been saving for! God was taking care of Bertha as well.

During this time we had been praying for Jeff and Holly, our next door neighbors from Wisconsin. They had let us know several days after we had moved in that we could be good neighbors as long as we didn't *shove Jesus down their throats*. So we agreed that we would never talk to them about Jesus...unless they asked!

I came out one morning to find Jeff under the hood of their car. It wouldn't start and he would surely be late for work. I tucked my necktie into my shirt (some of you remember when preachers wore ties nearly 7 days a week) and got under the hood with him. His battery cables were so corroded that no power could get through. I grabbed what few tools I owned, cleaned off his cables, gave him a jump start, and sent him on his way. No, I didn't say a word about Jesus. I just found a way to demonstrate the love of Jesus that day. From time to time Holly would ask Debi to watch their baby so she could run errands or visit her doctor. Again, no talk about Jesus, just a demonstration of his love.

Late one evening Holly showed up at our door in tears. Jeff had stopped at a bar on his way home from work and now he was passed out in a booth. A friend had phoned Holly. He was right there with Jeff and could give him a ride home - but who would drive their car home (this bar was about 40 miles away)? So there stood Holly - angry with Jeff and wondering how to get their car so he could get to work the next morning. Debi agreed to watch their baby while Holly and I headed to the bar in our car. When we arrived at the joint, we found Jeff and, sure enough, he was passed out drunk. Together we dragged Jeff into the back seat of their car, and I followed as Holly drove him home. Once we arrived at home, I helped her drag him in through their front door where we dropped him for the night. Again, no Jesus talk - just love.

We often heard them fighting and yelling through the thin wall that separated our apartment from theirs. The more they fought, the more we prayed. Then one evening - again, it was around 11:00 p.m. - there was a knock on our door. It was Holly, bawling her eyes out. We invited her in. As she poured out her problems, she asked, *Why does your marriage work so well? Why don't you ever seem to have problems....and why are you so kind to us?* I said, *We can't tell you, Holly, because we promised to never talk about Jesus - unless you asked!* She replied through her tears, *Well, I'm asking!* For the next 5 hours we prayed with her, took her through the Bible, and explained to her the way of salvation. We also shared testimonies of God's goodness and grace in our lives. At 4:00 a.m. Holly was on her knees at our couch, surrendering her life to Christ and asking Him to save her husband and their marriage.

She began attending the Tuesday night Bible study in our home, but could not attend Sunday services because Jeff refused to let her go. After several more weeks, during a Tuesday evening Bible study, there was a light tapping on our door. It was Jeff, wondering if he could join us. He had seen a dramatic change in his wife and wanted to know more about this Jesus. Several weeks later Jeff also surrendered His life to the only one who could change their family.

My agreement with the church was part time, although I was working at it full time! However, I had been asking God if I should still be doing more. One day an older couple from the church asked me what I would do if I had a rent-free building available. This building had at one time been their cafe, but now it was standing empty. They had spoken with several interested buyers, but sensed that they were supposed to hang on to it. I told them that, if it were mine, I would open up a Christian book store. They agreed to let me have the building rent-free for three years. After that we could negotiate a contract. They would also provide resources so that I could repaint and replace the carpet. As work progressed on the building, I was also writing letters to various distributors seeking to open accounts with them. I had no money, but since I was determined to begin small and stay out of debt, every letter that I wrote received a positive response! At first several of the suppliers agreed to send product to me on a C.O.D. basis only. No problem! I began to order merchandise with every spare dime we could find. Others heard what we were doing and gave us some generous offerings!

Within a few months we opened up Sonlight House Christian Book Store. Since the building had been a cafe, I left three booths in place. I served fresh coffee every morning and invited our first few customers to stop in anytime for a cup. Soon several bank employees started bringing their lunches to Sonlight, perusing some of our books while sipping on free coffee! They often bought those books before heading back to their places of employment. I also offered a discount to churches and to any legitimate Bible study groups. The closest Christian book store was ten miles away in Walla Walla, WA. However, since there was no sales tax in Oregon, I had a price advantage over them. Furthermore, they did not offer the discounts that I promised. With every dime of profit I would order more product. Soon the shelves began to fill up, and life was great!

To bring a phone into the store required a $50 deposit. Every time I got $50 ahead, I chose to pour it back into more product. We used our home phone number for the business, and several times a day Debi would bring me my messages (do you remember when there were no cell phones?). To return calls and to place orders I would run across the street to the phone booth outside the Shell gas station. One day a customer came in just as I was exiting the phone booth. She wondered if the

Don Bergstrom

store phone was out of order. I explained to her my dilemma. When paying for her purchase, she added $50 to her check and told me to order a phone! Praise the Lord!

Billy Graham's book on the Holy Spirit was the hot Christmas item that year. I had ordered a good supply, but by noon on December 24 I was out! A woman came in to purchase a copy and was disappointed to learn that I had no more in stock. Then I had a bright idea. If she could stop back in around 3:00 p.m. I would have a copy of that book for her! She was amazed, and agreed to return. I quickly called Debi, asked her to grab the kids and come mind the store. I then drove on some very treacherous, icy roads to Walla Walla, bought three copies of the book (paying retail price) and returned before 3:00 p.m. Not only was that woman thrilled, but before the day was over I had sold those other two copies (I should have purchased even more)! Incidentally, the amazed woman was the Sunday School Superintendent of a rather large church in town, and soon was bringing all of their business our way!

When I wasn't waiting on customers, I was either studying for the next Bible lesson at church or ministering to those who would pour out their problems over a cup of that free coffee. From time to time some of the women from our church would stop by with plates of fresh cookies, something all of our customers loved!

One day the interim pastor asked if I would be willing to serve as the senior pastor of the church. I argued that I really didn't know how to be a senior pastor, but he assured me that, if I would just keep on doing what I was doing, things would work out. Pastor Howard Baker in Walla Walla agreed to be my mentor, and soon walked me through the process of becoming licensed as a minister of the Church of God.

Now I had another problem! Both the church and the business were growing, so I now had two full time jobs. Some weeks it was not easy to keep up. So we began to fast and pray.

Our Journey With Jesus

Should I be a pastor or a retail merchant? One morning as I was waiting to hear His voice, the couple that owned the building came by. After pouring up a cup of coffee and grabbing a few fresh cookies, they asked if we could talk. Understanding my dilemma, they wondered if I would be willing to sell the Christian book store to them. Since they already owned the building they would just be buying the merchandise and fixtures. That was my answer! We took inventory, added up the value of everything in the store, and agreed on a price. They headed to the bank and within an hour returned with a cashier's check. I was now a full time pastor at the First Community Church of God just down the street. And I was finally receiving a salary.

Our fourth child, Luke, was born while we were serving there. He was our third home birth. During that pregnancy Debi began to hemorrhage. Knowing that she might lose our baby, we asked others to join us for a time of persistent prayer and fasting. Like any good doctor, I also put Debi on bed rest! Once again, prayers were answered and Luke was born, healthy (and quite handsome).

With our growing family it was becoming obvious that we needed a bigger car. The money from the sale of the Christian book store gave us the resources to buy such a car. I looked at a Chevy station wagon, and the church rejoiced with me when they heard that I found a great deal on such a nice family car! But I also had my eye on a red 1968 Ford Galaxy 500 convertible! It belonged to a mechanic at the Ford garage. Since he had just lost $2,500 in a poker game, he was willing to sell this classic rag top for the same amount so he could replace the funds in their saving's account before his wife discovered the withdrawal! Because of the bench seat in the front, I could easily fit my family of six in this beauty! And, unlike a Chevy wagon, this car would surely appreciate in value.

Don Bergstrom

But what would the church think? Little old ladies on Social Security were making sacrifices so their pastor could draw a salary, and now he's cruising around in this red convertible? A station wagon made sense, but this flashy car?

I just happened to be preaching through the book of 1 Corinthians. In chapter 8, Paul was talking about eating food that had been offered to idols. Paul himself didn't have a problem with this, but weaker Christians could stumble in their walk if they saw Paul doing this. So in verse 13, Paul said, *Therefore, if what I eat causes my brother to fall into sin, I will never eat meat again, so that I will not cause him to fall.*

My contemporary illustration that morning was the convertible. The red Ford would be a better investment than the Chevy wagon, but if my driving that flashy convertible around would be offensive to anyone in the church, I would choose the wagon. I then invited the church to share their thoughts with me after the service was dismissed. Most thought the red Ford convertible was a great option. Some had even noticed it on the used car lot, wishing it could be theirs!

Ultimately, there was just one elderly couple that I was concerned about. They had given so much to the church, and I was sure that they would see me as being too worldly if I chose the rag top. And, sure enough, that morning they were purposely lingering until everyone else had departed. *Oh no,* I thought, *here goes my dream car!*

As they approached me, I noticed that she had a twinkle in her eye! *If you'll put the top down and give us a ride to the drive-in restaurant, we'll treat your family to ice cream cones! You see, we've always wanted to ride in a convertible, but we've never known anyone who had one!*

On Monday morning I bought the car. On Monday evening we put the top down and took this couple for the ride of a lifetime. And, yes, they treated all of us to ice cream!

Our Journey With Jesus

With the birth of our fourth child, it was also true that our two bedroom apartment was getting a bit crowded. The church was growing, and the Board came to me one Sunday and told me to look for a bigger place. They had been paying our $225 monthly rent and said we could spend up to $350 on a rental home. Praise the Lord! We began searching…but nothing that we looked at seemed to be right.

Several months later as I was praying, I sensed the Holy Spirit asking, *Do you believe I have a home for you? Yes, I could believe it – we just weren't finding it!*

If you believe it, then why haven't you given your landlord notice – and why aren't you packing?

The next morning I went to our landlord with our 30-day notice. Knowing how crowded we were, he was glad for us. He then asked where our new rental home was. I explained that we hadn't found it yet, but giving notice was our step of faith. He just shook his head and said, *Okay. I'll call the next person on my waiting list…if you're sure!*

We began to pack as we searched even more diligently. Those 30 days sped by! It was a Friday morning, and our landlord had a new family waiting to move into our place the next day! Several folks from the church showed up to help us move out – yet we had no place to go! *I guess it's time to pray,* said one of the saints.

As we prayed together, the phone rang (good thing we hadn't made the final call to have it disconnected). The caller was a Christian realtor in our town. They had built a home to sell, but since it was not selling, they had just decided to rent it out. They had no clue that we were looking, but thought we might know a responsible Christian family that could rent their brand new home.

Well, we're looking, but I know where your home is – and I'm quite sure it's way out of our price range. When I explained that we could only pay $350 per month, he said he would speak with his wife and call me back. Within 30 minutes he called and said we could have it for $350. *How soon would you like to move in*, he asked. *Well, would ten minutes from now be too soon?*

As the men from our church sped over to the home with the first load, several of the women began to clean our apartment. By the end of the day we were all moved in and our apartment was ready for the next tenant. Once again God came through!

Shortly after completing our third year in ministry, I received a letter from a church in California asking if I would come and be their associate pastor. We sure didn't want to leave Oregon! The church had grown to over 90 in attendance, Larry, the band teacher, was leading our worship services, they were paying me a real salary, and were willing to help us buy that brand-new 3 bedroom home that we were now leasing. No, we didn't want to leave! But we agreed to fast and pray about this request.

Within two months we were headed for Pacific Grove, CA, to meet with the pastor and congregation there. Soon we were headed back to Oregon to resign and pack up our stuff so we could move to California. We just had one slight problem. Although the church in California offered us more money than we had been receiving in Oregon, rental prices on that beautiful Monterey Peninsula were also a lot higher than that $350 home we had grown to love in Oregon! In fact, the first rental we looked at, which was practically under a freeway overpass (I thought the price on that one should be within our budget) was $1,050 a month. This would practically take all of our new California compensation!

Did we miss the Lord? How could He send us to a city we couldn't afford to live in? Once again, as an act of faith, we planned to begin our journey to California in just two days… not knowing how we would make it financially! Pastor Elroy

Our Journey With Jesus

Weixel in Pacific Grove had asked us to call him before we hit the road so the church could be praying.

Oh, by the way, he said, *a couple in the church is moving, and they are offering you their Pacific Grove home...rent free!* Several days later we moved into our beautiful California home, complete with a fenced-in yard for the kids!

On April 1, 1980, I began serving as their associate pastor and continued to learn under this seasoned, caring pastor. On December 1st of that year Heather, our fifth child, was born. Another home birth, she came into this world in the master bedroom of our home.

One day God called that seasoned pastor to Indiana, and by mid 1981 the congregation asked me to stay and serve as their senior pastor. After a time of prayer and fasting, I said yes. Since I still had no formal training, I enrolled in a continuing education program through the Anderson University School of Theology. I chose courses that would continue to prepare and equip me for the ministry God had gifted me for and called me to.

We loved Pacific Grove! Our older children were soon attending David Avenue Elementary School, which was located right across the street from the church. We also opened up our home to a Vietnamese refugee. She had most recently been in Indonesia as an unaccompanied minor, and soon TT became part of our growing family.

Using the Navigator's book, *God Can Make it Happen*, I was teaching a Wednesday evening Bible study on the subject of faith. Early on in the study I asked all participants to write their *faith goals* down on a blank 3 X 5 card. These were things that only God could do in our lives. For some, it was an unsaved son or daughter. For others, a troubled marriage, a need for a financial breakthrough, or a plea for divine wisdom and guidance.

Don Bergstrom

I was suffering with a hernia. Since we still had no medical insurance, and since a hernia surgery was not in our budget, my *faith goal* was to hear from heaven concerning this need. I knew that Jesus could either heal me, or somehow provide the necessary resources. But, bottom line, whatever happened would only happen because of Him.

That evening I gave the group an opportunity to (voluntarily) share their faith goals so others could be praying with them. I also shared my need. Following the study one man approached me with a question. Since I had once served in the U.S. Army, *had I thought of going to the V.A. Hospital for help?*

Great idea! Trouble is, my six years were spent in the Army Reserves, and once I received my honorable discharge, no benefits were available. The next Sunday, the Board of Trustees asked to meet with me. Since the congregation was growing and doing well financially, they wanted me to get some quotes for a medical policy for my family. As I met with one agent, I explained to him why the Trustees were so eager to do this. However, as I already knew, my hernia would not be covered by any policy since it was a preexisting condition. Then the agent asked, *Have you ever been in the military? If so, maybe the V.A. could help you! A*gain I had to explain the difference between an R.A. (Regular Army guy) and an E.R. (Enlisted Reservist). He suggested that I try anyway! So I wrote a letter to the V.A. Within a few weeks I heard back from them. Since I was only a Reservist, no benefits were available. Yes, I already knew this.

Several days later I received another letter from the V.A. If I called the phone number in the letter, they would schedule an appointment for a physical! I called for clarification!

No, I was not available for any *disability* benefits! In other words, I couldn't ask for a big check, stating that I had not been able to work for the past ten years because of my condition! But I could come in for a physical to determine whether or not I needed this surgery!

The examining doctor soon discovered that I really did need surgery, and sooner than later. I went to the office down the hall to schedule a surgery date. I once again explained to the person behind that desk that I was not an R.A. and that I didn't think Reservists could actually receive this benefit. She agreed, yet stated that, *if the paper work says you can have surgery, then you can have this surgery! After all, the Government is never wrong!*

The following week, as I lay in the hospital recovering from surgery, a woman from the medical office came to visit me. She explained that there had been a mixup in the office, and that I was not eligible for the surgery after all. However, since it was their error (apparently the typist was so used to typing in R.A. and not E.R., that it was her typing error that started this whole ball rolling), I would be free to go home without any surgical cost to me! However, now that they had discovered the error, I would have to at least pay for an office visit when I returned to have the stitches removed.

Well, praise the Lord, there's more to this story! On the morning I was supposed to have surgery, I was the first patient on their list. However, when they took my temperature, it was slightly elevated (I think it was because the Mormon in the next bed gave me his cup of coffee, and added to my own cup, caused my temperature to read slightly higher than normal). So instead of being the first one on hernia row for surgery that day, I was the last. Medical students from nearby Stanford University apparently needed a guinea pig. They chose me, their last surgery of the day, as their experiment with dissolvable stitches! So no need to ever return! Even though the Government really was wrong this time, I did offer to find a way to pay for the surgery (I don't believe in taking advantage of anyone), but was told to just enjoy the blessing! As I told

Don Bergstrom

this story to our Wednesday night class, all were encouraged to continue believing God for their own miracle!

On Sunday mornings I was preaching a series of messages from 1 Corinthians 13, the love chapter. One Saturday evening as I drove home from my office, I was very pleased with the message the Holy Spirit and I had just completed for the next morning. *Love is patient, love is kind...*

When I pulled up to our home, I was shocked to see a huge pile of branches right in the middle of our driveway! Who on earth would have put them there? I walked into our home and asked Debi what she knew. Apparently the branches from a tree in our yard (right at the fence line, but still on our side) were interfering with the satellite dish on the roof of the neighbor's rented home. So that neighbor trimmed our tree for us - angrily cutting the branches so far back that it really ruined the looks of the tree. And, since it was "our" tree, he had decided that all those cut branches also belonged to us! What a huge mess he left for me to clean up! Suddenly the sermon I had prepared for the next morning didn't sound so good. *Patience? Kindness?* Right now *murder* sounded like a better theme! The next morning as I began the message, I explained what had happened the night before. Then I asked this question; *How many of you have a nasty neighbor? Many* hands were raised! Barking dogs! Loud music! A car that had been up on blocks in the next driveway for several months! The list went on...

It turned out to be one of the best series I ever preached there, because now we had sermons that we could actually put into practice. I exhorted all to forgive and begin praying for our neighbors, looking for ways to demonstrate the kind of love found in 1 Corinthians 13.

Several weeks later as I headed out the door for my office, sure enough, there was my nasty neighbor - under the hood of his car (I immediately thought of what had happened in Oregon not many years earlier). I breathed a prayer, asking for a fresh outpouring of the Spirit's grace (I surely needed it). I then approached that neighbor. *Troubles under the hood,* I asked? Sure enough, another case of corroded battery cables. Again, I repaired this neighbor's car without ever even mentioning his tree trimming a few weeks earlier. He mumbled something that kind of sounded like a thank you - and then drove off. We continued to pray, sought to be friendly, and invited them to a few events at our church. However, unlike our neighbors in Oregon, we did not ever see any visible answers to our prayers for these neighbors.

Knowing that we needed to discover God's specific plan and purpose for the congregation, I asked that we cancel all evening activities and services for one month. I would be at the church every evening and urged others to come and join me as we prayerfully sought His voice. During those 30 days I attended a meeting with other pastors from the area. Over lunch they began to talk about (and complain about) all the military personnel in the area. Fort Ord, the Naval Postgraduate School and the Defense Language Institute (DLI) all called the Monterey Peninsula their home. *Once you get these soldiers saved and teach them to tithe, they move on,* was the complaint!

I met with our prayer warriors that evening and suggested that we become a church that really cared about the military! After all, if we really could see them come to Christ, and if we really could teach them to tithe, we could then send them out as missionaries around the world! We now understood our purpose, and we began to act on it!

Since DLI's graduations were always held on the last Friday of the month, we scheduled a farewell for any graduates on the Sunday before the last Friday of each month. Folks began to open their homes on Sundays, inviting any military personnel in attendance that morning to their home for lunch. We planned marriage workshops for military couples, went door to door in areas where many in the military lived, inviting them to our services, and soon began baptizing those who were being saved. One Sunday after our worship service, we headed to the beach where more than 20 were baptized! It was also my privilege to perform weddings for several military couples. Ministry was exciting, and the church was growing! On Easter Sunday of 1985 we had to set out folding chairs to accommodate our growing attendance. Although we had only been in Pacific Grove for just over five years, our family knew that we wanted to stay there forever!

Chapter Seven
Do you know the way to San Jose?

One Tuesday evening in May of 1985 I received a call from the search committee at the San Jose (CA) Church of God. Had I ever thought about leaving Pacific Grove? My answer was a resounding *NO*. Would we be willing to pray about such a move?

Several weeks later we agreed to drive to San Jose to meet with the search committee. Everything within us hoped this would not work out! They were looking for someone with a PhD! I had no degree! They were hoping for someone in their early 50's – thinking that person could still relate to the younger generation, but could also stretch forward to the senior saints. I was 38! In fact, I did not fit *any* part of their profile! Praise the Lord! Perhaps *now* they would leave us alone!

By the end of that summer we were moving to San Jose. The church gave us an interest-free loan of $35,000 to help us get into the California real estate market, and did not expect any repayment unless and until God would call us away someday. The only home that fit our profile had a swimming pool (the one thing that *wasn't* on my list), but it proved to be a blessing. When we priced swimming lessons for six kids, I was shocked. So one morning I promised a dollar to any kid who could swim across the pool by the time I would return that evening. All six were waiting to collect their dollar when I arrived at home. Then I promised two dollars to anyone who could swim across and back again. By the end of the next day they all collected their money. So $18 paid for all the swimming lessons our six children would ever need!

The church began to grow and our family was also about to do the same! One day Debi received a call from her mother letting us know that Debi's cousin was in prison. Would we be willing to care for his two year old son? Levi came as a foster child. While we continued to care for him, the courts eventually terminated both biological parents's parental rights. We then started the slow process to adopt Levi. He was eight when he officially became a Bergstrom.

San Jose turned out to be a real blessing for us in many ways and we all planned to stay there "until Jesus comes." The kids were making friends, my niece became our youth leader, and Debi began to work as a contract instructor for the American Red Cross. Yes, God was good and life was wonderful.

During one very rainy Friday night wedding rehearsal, a homeless guy named Glen entered our sanctuary. He was wet, cold and hungry, and wondered if we had something he could eat. Following that rehearsal, I took Glen into the church kitchen and heated up something from a can for him to eat. Because I was about to be late for the rehearsal dinner, I encouraged Glen to eat fast - and then invited him to our Sunday worship service. Since it was potluck Sunday, I promised that he would find a good hot meal, and that he would meet people who would love and care about him.

Sure enough, Glen came and brought a group of other homeless folks with him. I was really proud of our congregation for extending such a warm welcome. Glen continued to attend and the saints continued to love him. One day he came down to the altar following a worship service and surrendered his life to Jesus Christ. Since we had already scheduled a baptism for the following Sunday, I encouraged him to attend the baptism class that Wednesday evening. During the class, he asked if we used robes when we baptized. I explained to him that we were not that formal. *Just wear something you can get wet in - and bring a change of clothes with you.*

But Glen really wanted to wear a robe (he had seen a baptism many years ago, and they used robes). So I told him that, if he wanted to wear a robe, that would certainly not be a problem. He found a tattered terry cloth robe at the thrift store, and I gave him a couple of bucks so he could buy it.

Our baptistery was built into the platform. Under the pulpit was a big cover, and under that cover was the baptistery. That Sunday morning we would baptize about twelve new believers. Glen was the final candidate. When I called his name, he proudly walked across the platform, sporting his new terry cloth robe. Then, just before descending into the baptistery, he took that robe off (I guess he wasn't paying much attention when attending that baptismal service years earlier)! All he was wearing now was a pair of extremely tight fitting Speedos - and his many tattoos! Old ladies gasped! The youth began to snicker, and I pulled him down into the water as fast as I could. After baptizing him, I asked him to remain with me in the water. Since he was the final candidate, I dismissed the service with a prayer and a farewell. Only after the congregation turned around to head for the door did I dismiss Glen. Years later those who attended that baptism are still talking about Glen and his Speedos.

For his baptism we bought a Bible for Glen, complete with his name engraved on the cover. Someone in the church gave him a job, and Debi and I invited him to come and live with us. One Sunday morning I announced that we were starting a fund so we could buy some dentures for this toothless new believer. Now it was Sunday evening and I was doing some reading before retiring for the night. From down the hall I heard the pitter patter of small feet. It was our son Luke. Although he should have been sleeping by now, he was sobbing while holding out his little wallet to me. *Take it*, he cried.

Don Bergstrom

I knew he had been saving up for a sleeping bag, since the kids at church camp had teased him the year before about his Snoopy sleeping bag. Between his deep sobs, I thought he was saying that someone had *taken it* (his money). Surely our new friend Glen would not have done such a thing, nor would any of Luke's siblings. As I took Luke up into my lap, I realized that he was saying *take it! Take my money so we can buy teeth for Glen!*

Oh, Luke, don't cry. We can let the adults give the money for the teeth. Through his sobs he said, *that's what I've been telling Jesus for the last hour! But He wants me to give My money to Him!* I took the money - all of it - and added it to the collection. Within just a few weeks Glen was grinning ear to ear, showing off his new teeth!

After about a month Glen asked if he could take Luke for a walk one evening. Since we had grown to trust this guy, we agreed. Glen and Luke walked to a nearby sporting goods store where Glen bought Luke the best sleeping bag he could find! You see, even though I thought Glen was sleeping, he had heard my conversation with Luke that Sunday evening!

In time Debbie, our youth leader (and my niece) would marry Jerry, the Chair of the Board of Trustees. Since she wanted to devote her time and energies to being a wife and homemaker, it was time to search for another youth pastor. As we fasted and prayed, I began to sense that Ron Hunt was God's choice. Ron was once in our youth group in Pacific Grove and had recently graduated from Anderson University in Anderson, IN. I called him and, although he was glad to hear from me, he informed me that he was now working for Sandi Patty (booking her concerts and managing her tours) and did not feel called to leave that position.

Months went by, yet I continued to believe that Ron was God's choice for our congregation. I even sent him a few letters, urging him to sincerely seek the Lord concerning this matter. During one Saturday meeting of the Church Council, the subject came up again. Most agreed that we really needed to get serious about hiring a youth pastor! Again I explained that Ron was that person, and that he needed to hear from heaven! One of our Church Council members made a suggestion. They should all get down on their knees and begin to pray - and I should go back to my office and call Ron once more. Ron answered the phone, and when he realized who was calling, there as a very long pause. *Ron? Are you there?*

Don, I just knew you would be calling today. When do you want me to move to San Jose? He then asked me if I had heard about the fire. Sandi's warehouse and office complex had burned to the ground not many days earlier. When the Fire Marshall finally gave her employees permission to go in to see if they could salvage anything, Ron discovered that everything on top of his desk was history! As he opened the desk drawers, he also discovered that the heat had even charred the papers in those drawers. All was lost, except for one letter in a bottom drawer! Sure enough, it was the last letter he had received from me. Through that discovery, he came to believe that God was calling him to leave Anderson, IN, for his new home in San Jose, CA.

Early in 1993, Debi and I attended a ministers' meeting in Sacramento. A couple from the Clairemont Church of God in San Diego asked to meet with us after one of the conferences. *Had we ever thought about leaving San Jose?* **NO!** *Would we be willing to pray about it?* What could I say? So, as promised, we began to pray, although our prayers were certainly not in earnest.

Six months later they called, wondering where our resume was, as they had been waiting for us to send it. I told them that we had not even considered sending a resume, because we didn't think it was time for a move. Would we pray some more?

Don Bergstrom

After a season of prayer and fasting, we headed to San Diego for an initial interview with the search committee. A second trip would soon follow, at which time we would officially candidate. We came home, presented our resignation, and put our home on the market to sell.

A recession had just hit the Silicon Valley, so home prices were down and sales were very sluggish. We left five of our kids in San Jose with Debi's parents, and took two of them with us to San Diego. We would be staying with a family in the church while we waited for our home to sell. They had room for four of us. Since Jason would be starting his senior year of High School, we took him with us and, since Heather would be starting Junior High, we also took her.

Ministry in San Diego was going well, but our home in San Jose was not selling. And we were sure missing our kids! On my walk one morning I spotted a 5-bedroom home for rent. Perfect! I called our realtor, asked him to find a renter for our unsold home, and signed a lease on the home in San Diego. We made a trip back up to San Jose to get the rest of our belongings – and our other five kids! We celebrated Thanksgiving in our newly leased home in San Diego, and gave thanks to God for the fact that our San Jose home was now rented out.

After a year, our lease in San Diego was up and the owner wanted to sell the home. We made her a reasonable offer, which she thought was too low (eventually she sold that home for less than we had offered). In the meantime we found another home, made an offer, and bought it just in time to celebrate Thanksgiving of '94 in it. Eventually our renters in San Jose moved on. They had thrashed our home, so our son Jason and I made a trip up there to do what we could, hiring other professionals to help us put it back in shape. I told the realtor that I wanted no more renters! Sell it!

Our Journey With Jesus

For the next six months that home stood empty. We now had two mortgage payments with no rental income to help us out! It was a tough time for us! Yet God continued to provide!

During that time the church sent us to a Church of God global mission's gathering in Sydney, Australia. All of our basic expenses were paid by the saints in the church, but because of our two mortgage payments, two property tax and insurance payments, and two utility bills coming in each month, we knew we probably would not be spending much money on souvenirs, etc. After attending a rewarding conference, our return flight to the U.S. stopped in Hawaii for a few days of fun. It was part of the package. In Hawaii the tour took us to Hilo Hattie's, a popular place to buy souvenirs. While everyone else was loading up on T-shirts and other Hawaiian treasures, we just looked around, secretly wishing we could buy some of these unique gifts for our seven children back home. After all, it was our first time in Hawaii, and who knew if we would ever get there again?

Just then a stranger walked up to me. He was not part of our group and had no way of knowing our situation. *The Holy Spirit is telling me to give you something.* With that, he shoved a $100 bill into my shirt pocket. I heartily thanked him as he walked away, disappearing into the crowd. Hilo Hattie's was having a sale on Hawaiian T-shirts and we were able to buy seven, plus a few boxes of Hawaiian chocolates for the several families who were watching our kids! God certainly cares about the things that concern us!

Eventually the San Jose home sold for a lot less than we had originally hoped. But God was still God and we believed that He knew all about our situation. He also more than made up for our losses the next time we sold a home. Read on to learn more!

We made several trips back up to San Jose for weddings. Our oldest son Jason married Kathy, a beautiful young woman

Don Bergstrom

from the congregation we had pastored there, and TT married Steve, a handsome young man she had met while attending college in San Jose. Since Kathy already had a daughter, we became in-laws and grandparents – all in the same evening!

We were falling in love with San Diego. The sunsets at La Jolla are still the best we've ever seen! As time marched on, eventually Michelle met Shawn and Rebekah met Duane. In 1998 both of these daughters married the godly men they were dating. Before long Luke met and soon married Abigail, another gift of joy and love added to the family.

During the summer between her junior and senior year of high school, Heather headed to Wyoming to work at Lone Tree Bible Ranch. Since they asked her to return, she headed back to Wyoming after her high school graduation. There she met Brad, and soon they were married.

In 2002, I sensed that another change was coming. After many days of prayer and fasting I was led to resign from the pastorate in San Diego. One hour before I met with our Church Council to present that resignation I received a call from Houston 1st Church of God in Texas. They asked if I would be willing to send my resume to them, and I did.

In time we met with the elders for an interview. Knowing that we were going to move from San Diego (although we still did not know where), we put our home up for sale. The sign went up in our yard on a Thursday morning just as I was headed to the L.A. area for a meeting. During the meeting my phone kept ringing, but since I was chairing the meeting, I just let the calls go to my voicemail. At noon we took a break and I checked my messages. All the calls were from our realtor, wondering where I was? When I returned her call she told me that multiple offers were coming in on our home (remember, the sign had only been up for 4 hours by now). The best offer was for $5,000 over our asking price. Debi was leading a tour on the east coast with American Christian Tours so, after

Our Journey With Jesus

making a quick phone call to her, I told the realtor to accept that offer. I met with her when I returned that afternoon to begin signing papers. Our home had just been sold in 4 hours for more than we were asking, and for more than twice what we had originally paid for it! We saw this as one more confirmation that a move was in our immediate future. Through this sale God also more than made up for our losses in San Jose.

We returned to Houston in July to candidate. We were convinced that God was calling us here, so we purchased a home during that visit even before the church body voted on us. We began ministry in Houston on Sunday, August 11, 2002.

I must tell you more about our move from San Diego to Houston and about the home that we purchased there.

Don Bergstrom

Chapter Eight

... everyone who has left ... children ... for my sake will receive a hundred times as much and will inherit eternal life.
- Matthew 19:29

By the time God was calling us to Houston, six of our seven children were married, Debi and I were being blessed with grandchildren (today we have twenty-six), and most of our family lived in California. Our last son, Levi, had also just moved out, so we were empty nesters with kids who would often come back home for special occasions like Christmas, Thanksgiving, birthdays and anniversaries. But now we were about to leave family and friends behind. Because of the many miles in between, we knew that we would not be able to see our children and grandchildren very often! Because our family was close, this would not be easy!

During one of our final evenings in San Diego we were driving up to nearby Ramona to say our final good-byes to our daughter Michelle, her husband Shawn, and their two precious children. As we drove along, we were listening to a song by Robin Mark on our CD player. That song expressed our feelings well.

Jesus, all for Jesus, All I am and have
and every hope to be
Jesus, all for Jesus, All I am and have
and every hope to be.

All of my ambitions, hopes and plans,
I surrender these into Your hands
All of my ambitions, hopes and plans,
I surrender these into Your hands.

Our Journey With Jesus

> *For it's only in Your will that I am free,*
> *For it's only in Your will that I am free.*
> *Jesus, all for Jesus, All I am and have,*
> *and every hope to be...*

Once again we were leaving behind everyone and everything that we loved, doing it all for Jesus. For, like Robin Mark, we had discovered long ago that our true freedom and ultimate joy is found only in the center of His will.

So when looking for a home in Houston, I convinced Debi that smaller is better, even though she wanted a larger house with room for family to stay if they could visit. Yet I reminded her that our family would no longer be joining us for those special times. We found what I thought was the perfect home for two.

Twenty-two months later Shawn, Michelle and their two children moved to Houston. Shawn's parents and grandparents couldn't stand to be so far from the two grandchildren that we had in common, so soon they came to Houston. Next, our youngest son Levi came. After a short stay he enlisted in the U.S. Army and left for basic training. In April of 2006 I flew to San Diego to drive a moving truck back to Houston for our oldest son Jason, along with his wife Kathy and their four children, and one or two extras they had with them. They moved in with us until they found a place of their own in nearby Montgomery, TX.

It was Mother's Day, 2006. We had invited a few widows to our home for lunch following the worship service that morning. Also joining us for lunch were Jason's family (still living with us), Shawn and Michelle with their kids, and Shawn's parents and grandparents. At least twenty of us gathered in our home for that feast. I began to realize that Debi was right; we should have purchased a bigger home when moving to TX! As I looked around that afternoon I silently said, *Lord, this house is too small! Why, we don't even have room around our table for all of our children!* After our guests were gone and only family remained, I called our realtor who lived three doors down. I invited her to our home for homemade cheesecake, but only if she would show us a larger vacant house down the street. During my morning walks I had noticed that it was for sale. As we walked through this place, all agreed that it would be more suited for our needs. So Debi and I began to pray.

The next morning my daily Bible reading took me to Psalm 128:1-6; *How happy are those who fear the LORD - all who follow His ways. You will enjoy the fruit of your labor. How happy you will be! How rich your life! Your wife will be like a fruitful vine, flourishing within your home. <u>And look at all those children! There they sit around your table - as vigorous and healthy as young olive trees</u>. That is the LORD'S reward for those who fear him. May the Lord continually bless you from Zion. May you see Jerusalem prosper as long as you live. May you live to enjoy your grandchildren (New Living Translation)*. It was one of those times when Bible verses leap off the page and speak to your heart. As I shared these words with Debi, we decided to make an offer on that larger home. Acceptance of our somewhat ridiculous offer would be the final confirmation of God's direction. On June 9, 2006, we moved into our new home.

Our son Luke, his wife Abigail, and their four sons moved to Houston in 2007. In 2011, our daughter Rebekah, her husband Duane and their three sons moved to San Antonio. Since that is only three hours from Houston, we are still able to get together with them quite often. And when our youngest son, Levi, finished his time with the Army he, along with his wife Vera and their son Sandon, continued to call Killeen, TX, their

Our Journey With Jesus

home. When my wife's mom went to be with Jesus in 2009, her dad (*pictured right*) moved in with us.

Wow, some days that larger home is still crowded! We also continue to open our door to those who are needy, in transition, or just traveling through. God has been good.

Chapter Nine

. . . go and make disciples of all nations . . .
- Matthew 28:19

During our years in San Diego, we made numerous mission's trips into Mexico. Working with a ministry called Samaritans, we helped erect church buildings. We also helped congregations in Mexico conduct Vacation Bible Schools. The church in San Diego supported a missionary couple in Venezuela, and they had recently visited our church. They encouraged me to bring a team from San Diego into Venezuela to minister in Cambalache, an extremely poor community behind the Puerto Ordaz city dump! Although I knew our time in San Diego was short, since news travels quickly in the Church of God, I couldn't tell them that I would soon be leaving and would, therefore, be unable to lead that team into Venezuela!

Once we arrived in Houston, I began to pray, asking the Lord of the Church (Jesus Christ) to show me what my focus in Houston should be. I sensed Him saying that I was to take the congregation out beyond the four walls of the church. After consulting with the Elders, I contacted our missionaries in Venezuela and began arranging our March of 2003 trip into that country. We worked on a building that would become home to the Cambalache congregation. We also conducted a Vacation Bible School and saw the Lord at work in many lives. In March of 2004 we returned to continue our work there. On our last evening in Venezuela I asked the missionary what the next project looked like. They planned to construct another church building in another area. They already had land, and several bivocational pastors could do the actual construction. All that was needed now was 14,000 U.S. dollars for materials.

Since we had just completed our annual Faith Promise mission's emphasis two months earlier, I just couldn't imagine going back to the congregation in Houston for another $14,000! Yet, as I shared the need with our team members (including three of our Elders) even before we left Venezuela, we sensed that we needed to somehow go home and raise the money.

On a very stormy Sunday evening following our return, we shared the need with our congregation. Because of inclement weather the turnout was slim, yet the enthusiasm was not. Within several weeks all the money was raised! Soon two fearless men from our congregation boarded an airplane with the pockets of their cargo pants stuffed with $14,000 cash (corruption in Venezuela prevented us from sending the money through the banks)! Not many months later I received some pictures of the new church building. It was filled with people who were hungering to know God's truths. A subsequent picture was of their first baptismal service. Yes, God was surely working in Venezuela!

Because of a growing hostility toward Americans, our missionaries were asked to leave the country which meant that our work teams would no longer be able to return. However, even today we continue to support the congregation in Cambalache with a monthly loose change offering called *Change that will Change Cambalache!* With our offerings the congregation is able to feed their congregants every Sunday, and it's the best meal most of them have all week. This free food also brings in guests who hear the Gospel before filling their stomachs.

In 2004 one of our guest speakers at Houston First Church was Dr. Bob Pearson. He was launching a new ministry to African AIDS orphans and had come to cultivate a relationship with our congregation. He encouraged the church to send me to South Africa and Zimbabwe for an August 2004 Vision Tour. A member of our congregation agreed to pay my way if he could go with me. Many in our congregation also began sponsoring AIDS orphans in Africa! (For more information about this ministry and to learn about child sponsorships visit www.horizoninternationalinc.com). I came home from that trip filled with a love for Africa and a desire to lead a team from our congregation back there the next year. Since then we have made several more trips to that continent with Dr. Bob. We also continue to support his work with prayer and finances.

As we were preparing for one of our trips to South Africa, Dr. Pearson asked Debi and me if we would prepare a Biblical teaching on sexual abstinence for junior and senior high school students. We also prepared six thousand commitment cards that students would be asked to sign. It is absolutely true that the only answer to this AIDS pandemic is sexual abstinence before marriage and faithfulness in marriage.

Charles, a pastor's son, became our chauffeur and translator as we began visiting schools in the Limpopo Province of South Africa. Since our presentation lasted only an hour we were able to travel to a number of schools each day. Debi would address the younger students and I the older. By the end of the week we had taught our mini-course to 5,551 students, and almost every one of them signed commitment cards! During the hours we spent in the car together, I continued to speak to Charles about his own relationship with God. Even though he had grown up in a pastor's home, he had never fully surrendered his life to Jesus Christ. On our final day together, I had the great privilege of praying with him as he invited Christ into his heart.

In 2009 Dr. Pearson invited Debi and me to participate in a pastor's conference in Zimbabwe. I would be part of a pastoral teaching team while Debi's role was just to love and encourage the African women and children. She is pictured here with just a few of the children we connected with while there.

One morning, right after I finished my portion of the teaching for that day, Tatenda, the leader of the churches in Zimbabwe, asked Debi and me to come with him. We got into his van and headed down the road. That's when he informed us that we were headed to an AIDS support group meeting and that my wife would be speaking to the group! Debi asked how much time she had to prepare for this meeting. *Ten minutes* was Tatenda's reply. In 2 Timothy 4:2, the Apostle Paul exhorts us to *be prepared in season and out of season.* Together we prayed for the Holy Spirit's guidance. By the time we arrived at the empty lot where the 82 women had gathered, Debi knew she was to speak about forgiveness. All of these women had AIDS and all needed to forgive the men who had infected them and the family members who had rejected them. She finished her talk with an invitation to step forward to pray a prayer of forgiveness. All 82 women responded.

Several days later, Tatenda called us out of the pastor's conference so we could return to the site of the support group. Debi was to speak again. When we arrived we found 302 men and women waiting to hear some Good News from the Bible. The Holy Spirit had prompted Debi to speak about the woman in the New Testament who had been hemorrhaging for twelve years (see Luke 8:43-48). When she reached out and touched the hem of Jesus' garment she was healed. Debi used this story to talk about the spiritual healing and forgiveness and acceptance that is available through the shed blood of Jesus on the cross. Sixteen people responded to her message as they prayed for this saving grace that only Jesus can give. Although we were soon on our way back to Houston, we learned that this group of 302 grew to over 2,000 by the weekend. Tatenda and his wife Lucia seized the moment by planting yet another congregation at this site.

Following the deadly earthquake in Haiti, I organized and led a team of volunteers from our church to Haiti in April of 2011. There we helped build homes for earthquake victims and ministered to the people who had suffered so much loss. One of the highlights of the trip was a foot washing service on our final day together. It was our intention to wash the feet of the leaders in the church, but when they turned around and washed our feet, the Holy Spirit's presence was felt by all.

For those in our congregation who have been unable to travel to Venezuela, Africa and Haiti, we began sending teams from Houston First Church into Mexico each year, building homes with Casas por Cristo. In time the violence on the border discouraged our people from traveling into Mexico, so in 2007 we traveled to East Texas with Habitat for Humanity to build homes for hurricane victims. In 2010 we traveled again with this ministry to Louisiana to help build more homes.

Kenya was our destination in 2012. I took a team there to begin rebuilding the Church of God Nora Hunter Memorial

Our Journey With Jesus

Hospital at Mwihila. One day the nurse in this picture approached my wife. She was a widow with three beautiful children. Because she and ten other hospital employees had not been paid in over eighteen months, she could no longer afford to feed her family. So, would we be willing to adopt her three children and take then to the U.S.?

Later I asked Dr. Douglas Wakhu to confirm her story. I also asked what it would take to pay those back wages. *About ten thousand dollars,* he replied. I presented the need to our ministry team. Later I shared her story with our entire congregation back in Houston. Within a matter of weeks the need was met. All of those hospital workers' back wages were paid in full! To God be the glory!

In Kenya we also ministered to about 400 pastors and church leaders, teaching on subjects they requested such as church discipline, conflict resolution, forgiveness, evangelism and more. Another team will return to the same project in 2013.

All this to say that we have sought to obey His command to take the church out beyond the four walls. However, not all of our focus has been on international ministry trips.

Don Bergstrom

We planted a Spanish-speaking congregation out of our building in 2007 and added an Arabic-speaking congregation in 2010. Since then all three congregations gather once a year for an International Feast and Worship Service. Only the Holy Spirit could create the kind of unity we are experiencing and that Jesus once prayed for in John chapter 17!

Chapter Ten

I tell you the truth, whatever you did for one of the least of these brothers of mine, you did for me.
- *Matthew 25:40*

Our preschool at Houston First Church took a hit following Hurricane Ike's 2008 visit. Since we had no electricity for about two weeks our parents had to find new places for their children and we never recovered. We soon made the painful decision to close our day care doors forever. We began to ask the Head of the Church what He would have us do so that we might continue providing ministry to those in Houston living just beyond our doors.

After a season of prayer, fasting, and meetings, we determined that our next task was to launch a new ministry to people on the street and other underprivileged people in our area. We would call it our H.O.P.E. Ministry (Helping Ordinary People Extraordinarily). Do you remember the lesson I learned when the pastor in Colorado shut the door in my face? From that day on I knew that any congregation under my care could never turn the poor and needy away. Since its birth in 2011, this ministry has continued to grow as faithful and caring volunteers from our church provide a weekly meal, showers, clean clothes and much love. We have also been able to help some of our H.O.P.E. family members find jobs, get off the streets, and get the medical attention they so desperately need. Because we also present the Gospel every time we gather, it has been our privilege to see some of them come to Christ and then follow Him down into the waters of baptism. We have also adopted an elementary school in our area where hundreds of students come from families living below the poverty level. Again our volunteers provide food for these needy families and more. Each Christmas we provide gifts for every H.O.P.E. family member, and gifts for the neediest families from the elementary school.

Since our major H.O.P.E. ministries take place on Thursdays, I brought a suggestion to our volunteers as we approached Thanksgiving Day of 2011. Assuming that our folks may want to be with their own families on that day, what if we provided a Thanksgiving meal and a time of worship for H.O.P.E. on Wednesday, the day before Thanksgiving? *Over my dead body* was the reply of one of our volunteers. The others were in total agreement! *If we can't minister to these folks on the real Thanksgiving Day, then how can we claim to love them?*

We fed more than 100 on Thanksgiving Day of 2011. Some of our guests wept as they told us what this meant to them. Many said it was the best Thanksgiving Day of their lives! By the time Thanksgiving of 2012 arrived, there was no thought of ever changing the tradition that began the year before.

Chapter Eleven

... the borrower is servant to the lender.
- Proverbs 22:7

Owe nothing to anyone - except for your obligation to love one another.
- Romans 13:8, New Living Translation

In chapter three I mentioned that, early in our marriage, we were convinced that God wanted us to get out of debt. Once we had sold or given away all that we owned we were, of course, debt free (it's easy to be debt free when you have absolutely nothing that you can call your own). When God began to give back to us, we continued to believe that we were to live the rest of our lives without ever going back into debt. Since that time, other than four mortgages in our past (we believe that a home mortgage represents an investment), we have lived debt free.

We have always sought to be, as the Bible teaches, generous with God and others. In return God has always been very generous with us! This is not about a Gospel of Prosperity (serve God and He will make you rich), but is about His commanding us to be good stewards of what we have in our hands. This is not to say that God doesn't make some of his obedient servants rich, but this is not a reason to serve Him!

I have told you just a few stories of how He has provided for us. If we sat down over a cup of coffee someday, Debi and I could tell you about a hundred more stories!

Sometimes we counsel others who are up to their ears in debt and struggling to survive.

One of our first questions is, *Are you being obedient with what God has already given you?* Obedience includes tithing (giving back to God through your church home at least ten percent of your income). After the tithe, we are also commanded to be generous with others in our world. This does not mean that we give to others indiscriminately. Indeed, sometimes the best help we can give others is to not give them more money, for they may not know how to handle it, or they may need to look to Him, not us, as their source.

Dear reader, are you a faithful manager of what God has blessed you with? You may be doing fine today without heeding what God's Word says about money, but a day is coming when we will all have to give an answer to his question; *What did you do with the blessings I sent your way?* My wife and I hope to hear these words; *Well done, good and faithful servant(s). You have been faithful with a few things; I will put you in charge of many things. Come and share your master's happiness (Matthew 25:23).*

Chapter Twelve

And we know that in all things God works for the good of those who love him, who have been called according to his purpose.
- Romans 8:28

I had already sent this manuscript to the publisher when my wife encouraged me to tell one final story. A friend named Larry Hott also believed that this book would not be complete without it. So our publisher graciously stopped the presses, allowing me to share one more account of God's goodness.

At the end of chapter three I told how we had taken a Holly Park mobile home in trade when we sold our home and how we gave that Holly Park to our church. But something else happened during those several weeks between the sale of our home and the giving away of the mobile home.

We had been traveling with Debi's aunt and uncle. Since they lived in a Bloomington, Indiana, mobile home park, I had a brilliant idea! What if we moved our mobile home from Buffalo, Minnesota, to Bloomington, Indiana? Because that's where our ministry seemed to be centered, it sounded like the perfect plan.

Debi's uncle Sonny knew an evangelist in Southern Illinois who had a mobile home toter for sale. Somehow Sonny came up with the thousand dollar asking price. We also knew a man who had a commercial driver's license named Larry Hott. Larry agreed to drive that truck from Illinois to Minnesota to pick up the mobile home and then tow it to Indiana. I warned him that this would be a bare bones trip since none of us were loaded with cash! As we prepared to drive away from the evangelist's property, he asked if we could give one of his *disciples* a ride to Minneapolis. We would be going right through the Twin Cities anyway, so we agreed.

It was cold and the truck had no heater. We soon gave that old white truck a new name; the Big White Bear. As the miles in that cold cab rolled by, we decided to stop for a hot cup of coffee. When the waitress asked if she could help us, the young man we were taking to Minneapolis replied, *No, but maybe we can help you! Do you know Jesus??* Larry and I were ready to crawl under the booth! Clearly this was not our style of *evangelism!*

We needed to go through Milwaukee to obtain permits for pulling that mobile home through Wisconsin. As the rain and snow began pouring down, Larry seemed a bit concerned when he noticed that the amp gauge on the dash indicated that our battery was no longer charging, but instead was showing a discharge. Debi's uncle always taught that *God is in every situation. If you want peace, all you gotta do is find Him there!* After we realized that the Big White Bear was having a problem, Larry and I began asking each other, *are you seeing God in this situation?*

We pulled into a gas station just outside Milwaukee. It was getting dark and running our lights was draining the battery quickly. We raised the cab up and tried to diagnose the problem. Meanwhile our *Jesus people* friend headed inside the gas station where it was warm. I glanced through the window just in time to watch him confront another unsuspecting *sinner*. I was glad, thinking that no one probably even knew he was with us! But then something amazing happened. Our friend and the stranger from Milwaukee were in the shop portion of the service station - on their knees - praying! Turns out that the stranger was putting just enough gas in his car to get a few miles out of town where he planned to blow his brains out! We later even saw his pistol on the seat of his car! When our young passenger confronted him, asking him if he knew Jesus, the man began to weep! No, he didn't know Jesus - but perhaps Jesus could help him make it through his hopeless situation. So that evening as he knelt on the greasy floor with our friend, he confessed his sin and his hopeless situation to Jesus and invited Him into his life! Our young friend's bold and blunt approach is exactly what this suicide-bound man needed!

Was God still in our situation? He sure was! If our failing alternator was somehow in God's plan for the saving of a soul, then we could deal with it.

Larry and I soon determined that our alternator was shot and needed to be replaced. We fired up the Big White Bear and headed for the nearest automotive parts store. Here we learned both the bad news and the good news. The bad news? The parts store did not have the alternator we needed, and it was just about closing time for every other parts store in the area. The good news? They could have an alternator for us first thing in the morning. Kevin, the young man at the parts store, offered to give us a ride to the nearest motel where we could spend the night. We had to explain to Kevin that we had enough money to either pay for a motel room - or buy an alternator. *You still got Him in that situation?* Larry whispered to me.

Kevin hummed and hawed for a bit, and then offered to let us crash on the floor of his apartment. We thanked him as we headed for his place. When we arrived, he explained our situation to his roommate, and that was not a problem. However, this roommate had just invited all of their friends over for a big drug party! *You still got Him in that situation?*

Kevin invited us to join the party, but we politely declined. Could we just hang out in Kevin's bedroom? We would sit around on the floor of his bedroom until the party was over. Kevin was fine with that, so we sat there having our own Bible study and prayer time. We needed to be reminded of God's promises from His Word (including Romans 8:28), and we sure felt like we needed to pray as well. Just as the party got rolling, Kevin came in and offered us a pizza and some soft drinks. Perfect!

As the party progressed, we found enough comfort in God's Word and enough humor in our situation that we ended up with a bad case of the giggles. After awhile Kevin came in to check on us. Why were we so happy? What were *WE* on? Our young evangelist told him that we were *high on Jesus!* Kevin wanted to know what that meant. So we began sharing the gospel with him. After he had heard all he was ready to take in, he headed back out to the party. But the Holy Spirit kept drawing Kevin back into our presence, and by midnight Kevin was on the floor with us, inviting Jesus Christ into his life!

The next morning Kevin prepared breakfast for us before we even woke up! As we drove back to the parts store, Kevin asked a favor of us. *Please don't mention any of this to my boss - because he really thinks Christians are weird!* It was sure cold that morning as Larry and I were out installing the new alternator. Since we had no tools with us, we ran back into the store a few times both to warm up and to borrow a few more wrenches. Each time we noticed that Kevin and his boss were in deep conversation. You guessed it!

Kevin had such a new joy and peace in his heart that he was soon telling his boss about us, about last night, and about Kevin's decision to become a follower of Jesus Christ.

Was God in our situation? Absolutely! But that's not the end of the story! The Big White Bear continued to have problems and, just before we crossed over into Minnesota from Wisconsin, the Bear gave one final growl, and then died! After it sat for about ten minutes, we prayed it into a truck stop. This time it stopped for good! We took a bus to Minneapolis and then called my cousin Bruce. He was kind enough to drive down to the bus station and give us a ride out to Buffalo. Our young evangelist also called a friend to come and pick him up. We never saw him again.

The next day I borrowed a truck from my brothers and headed back into Wisconsin to load up the Bear. We hauled it back to Buffalo and tried to find the problem. To make a long story short, the Big White Bear had reached the end of its journey. Where was God in *this* situation? Well, keep on reading.

I called Kevin to find out how he was doing. He had been telling everyone about his decision and was sure glad to hear from me. Could we come back to Milwaukee and share Jesus with his brother and sister-in-law? During this entire trip it began to dawn on me that maybe this plan to move the mobile home was not God's plan! I wanted the security of a ten thousand dollar mobile home for my little family, but God wanted me to find my security in Him. Back to the end of chapter four - this is when we gave the mobile home to the church. But God was not yet through working our situation out for good. After calling Sonny to let him know the fate of the Big White Bear, he told me to just find a way to get rid of it. Never mind the thousand dollars he had paid for it. The salvation of the man in the gas station and Kevin's new-found faith were worth more than an old white truck. Then I had another idea. I knew that our friends in Southern IL, Dick and Paulette, were in need of a car. I approached the owner of a used car lot in Buffalo and offered to trade the Big White Bear even up for a Plymouth station wagon that he had on his lot. He came over to examine the mobile home toter and decided that his mechanic really could fix it. We drove the Plymouth back to Illinois where this whole journey began and gave the car to our friends. They were sure praising the Lord for His provisions!

Was God still in our situation? Absolutely! But there's still more to the story. Before long my wife and I headed to Milwaukee to speak with Kevin's brother and his wife. Although they were attending a church, they were not fully committed to a vital relationship with Jesus Christ. However, that weekend, after hearing what Jesus had done for us and more recently for Kevin, they opened up their hearts completely to Him! Months later when we contacted them again, they were still attending the same church, but were now taking seriously what was being preached! Was God in our situation? Absolutely!

Dear reader, what difficult situation are you going through today? If you are not absolutely committed to following Jesus, why not turn your life - and your situation - over to Him right now? He really does care about you and your trials.

If you *are* committed to Him but cannot see Him in your present situation, remember the story of the Big White Bear. A broken down old truck and three broke occupants kept on looking for Him in our situation. When all was said and done, lives were changed for all eternity - and Dick and Paulette's prayers for a car were answered.

Several more comments about Romans 8:28 are appropriate here. If you will read the very next verse, you will discover what the *good* is that is spoken of in this passage. The good is that we will become conformed more and more to the likeness of Jesus Christ. You see, our trials are designed to grow us up! It's often been said that *God cares more about our character than He cares about our comfort!* Why? Because comfort is temporary, but character is eternal. And it's also been said that *God wants to turn our misery into our ministry*, and *out of our time of testing He will give us a testimony.* So believe that God is in *your* situation, and if you can find Him there - and follow Him through it - it will ultimately turn out for your eternal good and His glory.

Epilogue

For we are God's workmanship, created in Christ Jesus to do good works, which God prepared in advance for us to do.
- Ephesians 2:10

In my preface I stated that the above Bible verse is one that has shaped and guided my life. I am convinced that God created you and me on purpose and for a purpose. There are specific *good works* that each one is called to accomplish during our time here on earth. From the dedication page in this book, you know that my mom understood her purpose and pursued it with all of her heart.

Several years ago, while speaking on this verse to an audience of approximately 300 Christ-followers, I asked how many of them really believed that God had a specific plan for their life, including *good works* they were to accomplish during their years here on earth. Almost every hand in the place went up. Then I asked, *How many of you know what good works you were created to do, and can honestly say that you are living your life in pursuit of those works?* Less than 20 hands went up.

Dear reader, do you know why *you* are here on this planet? Do you know what *good works* God created you to accomplish and, if so, are you living each day in a way that will ultimately complete your purpose?

Long before Rick Warren taught the world about living a Purpose Driven Life, I had sincerely and earnestly asked the Father what my purpose for living was. Here is what I discovered: *I am here to . . .*

Love God, my family, my neighbors and my world in a way that brings glory to Him and blessing to them.
- Mark 12:30-31

Let His light shine through my words and deeds so that others might be drawn to Him and discover His gift of eternal life.
- Matthew 5:16

Lay all of my talents, time, gifts and earthly possessions at His feet to be used for His Kingdom's purposes.
- Luke 14:33

Lead as many as possible into a saving relationship with Him.
- Romans 1:16

It is my prayer that, as you read my story, you will be both challenged and encouraged. If you have never surrendered your all to Jesus Christ, I would encourage you to pause right now and, through a simple prayer, confess your sin to Him, invite Him to come into your heart, and determine that you will follow Him every day for the rest of your life.

If you profess to be His follower, yet you have never surrendered everything to Him, I would encourage you to read chapter five again. Then invite His Holy Spirit to fill you and daily control your life.

If you are discouraged today, may my story remind you that He is real, that He cares about you, and that He is able to meet you at your point of need.

May the grace of our Lord Jesus be with you
(1 Corinthians 16:23).

Our Journey With Jesus

www.ingramcontent.com/pod-product-compliance
Lightning Source LLC
Chambersburg PA
CBHW071404160426
42813CB00084B/468